From
STORY
to
ACTION

*Transform Your Storytelling to
Win Support and Ignite Change*

From STORY to ACTION

Transform Your Storytelling to Win Support and Ignite Change

Sally J. Perkins, PhD

Niche Pressworks
Indianapolis, IN

Author Photograph by: Megan Courtaney Photography

Published by Niche Pressworks; NichePressworks.com
Indianapolis, IN

ISBN
Hardcover: 978-1-962956-80-2
Paperback: 978-1-962956-79-6
eBook: 978-1-962956-81-9

Library of Congress Control Number: 2025913946

The views expressed herein are solely those of the author and do not necessarily reflect the views of the publisher.

TABLE OF CONTENTS

Preface

TOO MUCH FEEDBACK
TO IGNORE

On a hot July afternoon, I had no need for extra caffeine as I made the 125-mile drive home. I didn't need the caffeine, nor any music or audiobooks for that matter, because I was overflowing with energy after conducting a four-hour storytelling training with a cohort of physicians in a leadership-development program. Among the leadership skills they were learning was a component titled "Storytelling for Advocacy." This was my fifth year conducting the training, and every time the feedback was overwhelmingly positive. More and more so each year, in fact.

Participants would say things like:

> *"We were trained to think scientifically and never trained to think about how to convince people of the data in the form of a compelling story."*

> *"I wish I'd learned this a week ago before I had to go in front of the legislature to advocate for a public health cause. No wonder I didn't make the impact I wanted."*

"I was a skeptic about storytelling coming into this. Now I'm sold! So impactful and practical!"

"I'm not a great storyteller, so I'm not persuasive when I need to be, but these frameworks make it so much easier."

I also thought about the message I'd received from a physician after the previous year's training. She'd used the frameworks to tell a story to a patient and was astounded that the patient finally took the action she'd been urging him to take for years.

These comments swirled in my head as I drove. I reflected on the hundreds of groups I had worked with over the years, helping them champion their causes through effective storytelling. I reflected on the evolution of my storytelling frameworks — the Story Loop, Tree Tales, and Forest Stories. Due to the frameworks' specificity and simplicity, participants latched onto, applied, and remembered them long after the training.

While the market holds many great books on storytelling — books I recommend you read — the feedback I've received from my clients over the years indicates that the frameworks I offer provide something magically simple, yet powerful.

As I drove, it occurred to me: I love working with leaders who are advancing noble causes like public health, arts programs, youth development, community development, social services, customer service, environmental conversations, business process improvements, and so much more. I love watching them transform their ability to persuade their target audience. I love giving them simple storytelling frameworks to engage minds and inspire hearts. I love watching them shift from dread and confusion about their storytelling to excitement and confidence in which approaches will work best. I love watching their teams talk in "code" about the Story Loop,

Forest Stories, and Tree Tales, getting more strategic because of their newfound vocabulary.

If I die tomorrow, I thought, *these frameworks will become invisible and inaccessible to others who need to drive action around their worthy missions.*

At that moment, I decided to write this book.

My greatest hope is that no matter what cause you are championing, you too find these frameworks easy to use and transformative in your ability to tell compelling stories that inspire action and ignite the change you seek.

PART I

A Worthy
Cause Requires
Compelling Stories

Chapter 1

THE CHALLENGE

Why You Need Better Stories

What a noble cause you have there!
So, why can't you get the support you need?

THE STORY PROBLEM

In an early morning virtual meeting, Emily Bopp, chief of staff for a company called Empowered Ventures, and I were sipping coffee. I'd met Emily several years prior through a mutual acquaintance who brought her to one of my storytelling performances. We talked only a time or two after that, and I had hoped we might one day collaborate on a project because Emily was such a curious, forward-thinking, warm individual. She was always simultaneously smiling and contemplating.

"I need your help," she said. "Our company has a story strength and a story problem."

Well, this sounded right up my alley. Curious about the strength and problem contradiction, I asked, "What's going on?"

"Well, first off, we're extremely successful," she began, then paused as she took a sip of coffee.

Smiling, I replied, "You're definitely going to have to explain to me how that's a problem."

She laughed. "Well, that part isn't. The problem is that explaining our success to people so they, too, can become part of it is challenging."

"Ah, yes," I said, as her words were sounding even more in the vicinity of my alley. "What do you need from me?"

"Well, to start, it would probably help if I told you a little more about our company," she said.

She then began a remarkable story.

An Innovative Business Model Saves a Company

In 1974, Dick Hanzel and Dick Leventhal launched Top Value Fabrics (TVF), which sold different types of textiles to manufacturing companies throughout North America. In 2001, Dick became the sole owner. His slogan for the business was "We try harder," a mantra the employees lived out in a company culture that fostered personal accountability, high standards, and trustworthiness. This philosophy led to impressive business success.

As Dick entered his 60s, he began wondering what to do with the company upon his retirement, as he had no family heir to take the business. So, he started meeting with potential buyers — namely, investors and competitors.

But Dick soon realized that he didn't know these buyers, their values, or what they would do with the company, and he fervently wanted the company culture and success to live on. He and his employees, many of whom had worked there for decades, grew nervous about the future. They feared that buyers would drastically change the company, and the employees would lose control of their destiny.

Then, CFO Chris Fredericks proposed the idea of selling the company to the employees through an employee stock ownership plan (ESOP).

Employees as owners! Dick was both intrigued and skeptical. However, after much study and deliberation, he realized the ESOP trust would indeed allow him to retire and leave his life's work in good hands — the hands of his employees.

Dick took the leap. TVF established an ESOP Trust, which purchased 100 percent of the company's shares from Dick at a negotiated fair price, and soon all TVF employees became beneficiaries of the ESOP Trust.

When Dick and Chris announced the sale to the employees, they were, of course stunned, not knowing what to think. But Dick and Chris worked with the employees, helping them understand that with ownership, they would have a better financial future for their own retirements, and they would have a voice at the table in deciding how TVF could continue to thrive.

The New Model Takes Off

Within nine years, their ESOP plan met palpable success for both the company and its employees. TVF doubled sales and tripled profits, allowing the company to invest in new technology and acquire another fabrics company. Their workforce grew by 50 percent.

The first year or two after the conversion, employees saw minimal impact in their retirement account balances, but by years four and five, some of their balances exceeded what they'd been building in their 401(k)s for *years*. The increase allowed employees to travel extensively, retire earlier, and build financial security — just by coming to work and doing their jobs.

Employee engagement improved as they took ownership in saving the company money by, for example, devising creative ways to reuse shipping boxes rather than paying $35 for each new box. Whether working in leadership, in sales, or on the distribution floor, *everyone* was invested in the company's success.

As one of the long-time employees said, "Being employee-owned changed the whole dynamic of the company, a true 180-degree turn."

Adapting for Success: Empowered Ventures Is Born

But at the nine-year mark, a nagging concern weighed on Chris's mind. Their financial eggs were all in one basket. Knowing that all businesses go through ups and downs in the market, he wondered how they could protect the value they were building for their employee owners.

Then he wondered, what if TVF could build a diversified, employee-owned *holding company*? The holding company could invest in other successful founder-owned businesses and act as an investment office on behalf of the TVF employee owners and those of other companies. By expanding their net, they could offer more security for everyone.

So, TVF's board of directors made the decision to build a diversified employee-owned holding company — Empowered Ventures (EV) — which would acquire other businesses interested in the employee ownership model and give TVF an even bigger future. Within five years, EV acquired four additional manufacturing and services companies, successfully converting them all into thriving, employee-owned cultures within the EV ESOP.

Over $5 million has been paid out to Empowered Ventures' employee owners who retired or left the plan. Four other businesses besides TVF now have a secure future after their owners retired or are in the process of retiring. Employees are discovering new ways to contribute and grow, and they feel a profound sense of ownership and pride in their work and that of their coworkers and their company.

SOLVING THE PROBLEM: PUTTING STORIES TO WORK

After Emily shared this story, I took a deep breath. "Wow, that's amazing! What a noble enterprise!"

"Right?" she replied. "We're doing something incredible here. And when we approach prospective businesses for acquisition, our story has that same impact it just had on you. Investors and competitors typically talk numbers to prospects, but in our case, it's the *story* of employee ownership that convinces them."

"But here's the thing," she said. "Right now, only a handful of us can tell this story, and that's hampering our success. We just hired someone to conduct our marketing and communications efforts, but if we're going to bring more companies into our ESOP fold, we've got to equip more of our employee owners to be able to tell the EV story to hundreds of potential company owners. Moreover, we want them to be able to tell their *own* stories of success, which are far more compelling than ours."

Then she mentioned another problem. "When a company becomes employee-owned, many employees and potential hires are skeptical at first. They're reluctant to truly take ownership, not just financially but also by contributing to the vision and culture of the company. So, we need the employees to be able to tell their stories *to one another* to build a healthy culture of employee ownership."

Unfortunately, they had no system for ensuring that the EV story is or will be well told by others and no system for equipping their employee owners to tell their stories effectively.

This is why Emily had asked for an early morning meeting with me.

All of these factors were critical to the success of the ESOP model. Their absence would impede EV and its companies' success in several ways.

"Without more employee owners who are able to tell the EV story, we can't reach the hundreds of potential business sellers who would be attracted to the model," Emily said. "This will not only limit our ability to grow and diversify, but it will also prevent others from achieving the kind of success our incredible business model can bring.

"And it also hinders our culture's advantages," she went on. "Prospective and new hires need to hear stories of how other employee owners have made a difference in the company and benefited from the model. Without their examples, talented potential recruits may go elsewhere, not realizing what they're missing out on in this model. And newer employees may not feel comfortable leaning into the responsibilities of ownership. We need them to take part in decisions and offer feedback to shape the company's future, but without stories to show them how that works, they won't know how to do it or what's expected. They might not even believe they should. Over time, that will be a serious drawback."

Although EV had launched effective channels for storytelling (including a mini-documentary, a podcast, internal newsletters, and less formal videos for employee owners at Empowered Ventures' companies), they lacked a skillful approach to *personal* storytelling.

"This is why I really need your help," she said. "We have a summit coming up where about 40 employee owners who represent our different operating companies will be together for two and a half days. This would be an ideal time for some storytelling training.

"The employee owners who'll be present will range from production workers to marketing team members to HR, finance, and company leadership," she explained. "They come from vastly different backgrounds and experiences. So we'll need a way to help all of them to become equally confident and capable of telling the EV story broadly as well as their own stories to inspire their co-workers and new employees."

"Aha," I said, taking all of this in. "So what you're looking for is an actionable and repeatable process to teach these diverse stakeholders in your upcoming summit."

"Exactly," she said.

We quickly got to work. My two jobs were to 1) coach Emily so she could craft a codified version of the EV story and 2) teach her fellow employee owners actionable, repeatable processes, giving them the skills and shared vocabulary to collaborate in developing the best stories for their purposes.

Training Takes Hold

In just a few coaching sessions, the storytelling light bulbs came on for Emily. She had no trouble using the Story Types, the Story Loop, Tree Tales, and Forest Stories, as well as the other techniques you'll learn in this book. On the opening night of the summit, she used the frameworks to tell the attendees the Empowered Ventures story and their vision for the future. We then explained the power of storytelling, revealing exactly how Emily had crafted the story using the Story Loop framework.

Within minutes, all 40 people in the room, including senior leaders, office staff, sales reps, and employees representing manufacturing, distribution, construction, and trades, had united enthusiastically around three common experiences:

1. They knew the Empowered Ventures story and were both excited and inspired by it.
2. They were convinced of the need to tell their own employee ownership stories.
3. They already had a unique, easy-to-use tool for shaping a story.

Knowing we would reconvene the following morning for more in-depth training, I headed to my hotel room to get some rest.

At breakfast the next morning, the summit attendees excitedly told me that after dinner, many of them had gone to the hotel bar where (naturally) they started telling stories. They were proud to report that as they listened to one another's tales, they interrupted each other, saying, "Oh, look where you are in the Story Loop!" "I see the Loop in your story!"

I laughed, joining in their exuberance. I was thrilled to see they were already becoming aware of how they were telling stories, and because they had a common vocabulary for understanding how good stories work, they were naturally reinforcing the practice with one another.

Throughout that morning as we workshopped the storytelling frameworks and techniques, the teams crafted, shared, and refined their stories. Not only that, but they also began saying to one another things like, "I think we need to tell more Tree Tales at our monthly team meetings," and "I want us to have a Forest Story ready to share at our next annual planning session," and "Ooh! I can feel the power of the Story Loop when you say it that way!" They were already using the terminology they'd just learned that day (which, as I mentioned above, you'll learn in this book).

After just five hours of work, Empowered Ventures had a coherent framework and a common language for their strategic pillar of storytelling. Now, not just the marketing team, but *everyone* at the holding company and the key employee ownership champions at the operating companies were equipped to tell the right stories to the right audiences in the most compelling ways.

The Telling Results

Immediately following the summit, they put their new skills into practice to help employee owners from across the enterprise embrace a new initiative called Healthcare for Us. They generated both a Forest Story and several Tree Tales to drive home why the program mattered, to make the program "stick," and to persuade fellow owners to "lean in" to the initiative. They had hit the ground running.

And they haven't stopped. As I'm writing this book, Emily tells me that the company is now full of people who can tell the EV story. Leaders are now easily relating their own employee-ownership success stories, and employees have been inspiring their new and prospective colleagues with their own success stories. Emily is now much more confident that EV is fully equipped to write the next chapter of success for its innovative business model and its growing portfolio of companies.

YOU TOO HAVE A NOBLE CAUSE

If you are reading this book, you too are a leader — at any level in an organization of any type — for-profit, not-for-profit, government, education, or other — with a noble cause that needs to be amplified through effective storytelling.

When I say "noble cause," I'm referring to any vision of "something better" that you believe in and feel you must advocate for. That "something better" could be as grand as a vision for healthier air through reduced pollution, thus requiring monumental changes and government regulations in greenhouse gas emissions from airplane engines. Or it could be as small as a vision for better client engagement through a new protocol of a weekly email outreach from your customer service team.

Your noble cause as a leader might be internally focused in your organization, like making the lives of your employees better through an enhanced IT system, which means you must advocate for the necessary budget. Or your noble cause might be externally focused: Your objective could be to set up a food pantry in a particular location in your neighborhood, but you must convince external stakeholders to partner with you by sharing their space for you to run your food pantry.

There are no boundaries to what constitutes a noble cause. You must simply believe that what you are advocating for is worthwhile. Following are some examples from a wide range of industries.

Perhaps you work in **healthcare** as a public health advocate needing to convince legislators to change zoning rules to enhance food security in your community, or you're a physician trying to convince your patients to reduce their consumption of hidden sugars. Perhaps you oversee a patient services program in a pharmaceutical company and need to convince senior leaders to change medication access procedures in response to the feedback you've heard from patients.

Or maybe you work for a **nonprofit organization** as a fundraiser or marketer, needing to convince donors to support a capital campaign, or you need to recruit volunteers to help carry out your services, or you need to write grants for funding. Perhaps you're a leader in **higher education** needing to recruit students, improve alumni engagement, or secure funds for a new research laboratory, or you need to reverse the downward spiral of morale among your faculty and staff.

You could work in the **tech industry**, generating complex data on energy consumption, and you need to convey that data to stakeholders to shape the direction of energy consumption policies, or you want to influence how your employees understand and talk about the company's use of AI. Maybe you need to help your employees see the vision of your technology's potential to transform the transportation industry to benefit both humans and the environment.

Perhaps you work in **local government** as an agency head for child services, needing to unite your team around a new vision for the department and convince legislators to vote in favor of your budget increase request, knowing your request will compete with the requests of at least ten equally important agencies.

You may be a leader in *any* industry or any sector with a noble cause, big or small. Your mission may be internally focused for those within your business or organization, or perhaps it's externally focused for your stakeholders and those you serve. But whether your cause is big or small, internally focused, or externally focused, you will only influence others to see your vision and support your mission if you and your team are able to communicate it through compelling stories and have a cohesive system for crafting and telling the right stories for the right audiences at the right times.

THE PROBLEM IN COMMUNICATING YOUR WORTHY MISSION

No matter your leadership position or your cause, you are likely making statements like Emily's.

"We are doing something incredible here, but it's complicated, and we've got to figure out how to tell

*our story better because **our stakeholders just don't
understand it** and **won't do what we're asking.**"*

OR

*"We have the opportunity to do something impact-
ful here, but **we're not getting the support we need**
because our team isn't telling a consistent story."*

OR

*"We've got so much data to convey, but **our stakeholders seem disengaged when we share it. How
do we get them to act** based on what the data are
telling us?"*

OR

*"**I can't seem to motivate my teams** to comply with
this new procedure. How can I convince them?"*

OR

*"I'm not a good storyteller, but I have a sense that
**the best leaders are, which is why they get buy-in
from their people.**"*

In other words, you as a leader are, like Emily, up at night
wondering how you can motivate your employees to change
their behavior, how you can convince senior leadership to act on
your proposal for a process change, how you can inspire donors
to give to your cause, or how you can get your external stakeholders to understand and take action on the complex work you

do. You're wondering these things because you know that your audience's inaction will bring undesired consequences to your organization, your team, your business, and ultimately to those people whom you serve.

And though you, like Emily, may also have a sense that telling a compelling story is important, you may not be telling that story well for one of several reasons. Consider which of these obstacles resonates most for you:

- **You find yourself saying, "The way we're telling our story is not very compelling," but you don't know what to do about it.**

  You know your mission is compelling — you're just having trouble explaining it in a compelling way. This problem may simply be a matter of needing guidance on the structure of your story, the language you use, or what details you should or should not include and why. You may need techniques that can put your target audience in the palm of your hand, so they see the vision you want them to support.

- **You notice that no matter how strong your evidence is, when you share data in support of your cause, you're not getting much more engagement than some nods and a few questions.**

  This can be frustrating. Unfortunately, without a framework for guidance, it's often difficult to know how to share data in the form of a compelling story. You may be data-dumping inadvertently. Or the story may be clear in your mind, but not in the minds of your audience. You need story-weaving tools that can transform dry data into a message that will captivate, inspire, and ignite action.

- **You hear your audiences say, "I just don't get what you're trying to accomplish" when you discuss your mission.**

  Talking about one's mission without the clear structure of a well-told story can result in the vision sounding vague and complex to others. You need structures and tools that guide you to frame an explanation of something complex inside a simple, understandable, and relatable story.

- **You notice your audience doesn't seem to remember or prioritize your message.**

  If this is happening, the story you're currently telling could lack vital elements that make it unforgettable. If you've never given much thought to the kinds of details that are more likely to stick in an audience's memory, you won't know to include these elements.

- **Your team members lack a coherent vision of the story you're trying to tell and are communicating in different and haphazard ways that confuse your audiences.**

  This situation often occurs in large organizations. Perhaps your mission is broad or complex, so the marketing team is communicating about the laudable cause one way (or perhaps many ways if the team is large or has fragmented sub-groups), while the client success team is talking about it a different way, and the talent acquisition team is communicating in yet a third way. Without a unified approach that's easy for everyone to follow, your storytelling will result in watered-down, scattered messages that don't convey a coherent vision.

Poor Storytelling Impacts Your Success

No matter the obstacles, without a shared set of storytelling frameworks and a shared vocabulary for how you craft and strategize about your stories, you are at risk in three ways:

1. You, as the leader, cannot effectively cast *your* vision of the mission to your team.
2. Your team will remain fragmented in communicating and advocating for your purpose.
3. Most importantly: Your business, organization, or group will not obtain the needed support to advance your cause.

If you believe your cause is indeed noble and you want to obtain the support it deserves, you and your team, no matter how big or small, need a shared set of tools and frameworks to guide your storytelling. You need a common storytelling vocabulary that will get everyone on the same page in building a strategy for the types of stories you need to tell, the focus of those stories, and the ways you will tell those stories to make them as compelling as possible.

This effort cannot be left solely to the marketing team or the fundraising team or a communications team. Rather, you, as the leader, must equip yourself and your entire team with the same tools to successfully cast your vision to garner the support needed for your purpose. And the contents of this book can do just that for you.

A SPELLBINDING SOLUTION

If you believe your cause *is* indeed noble, you want your team sitting around the boardroom or even, like the Empowered

Ventures team, sitting around the bar at night, telling stories in the same compelling way. You want them strategizing about their storytelling using a common, unique vocabulary that has them all on the same page in their vision for using stories to advance the mission. **From Story to Action is a playbook of easy-to-use, proven storytelling frameworks that will transform your stories into strategic tools to captivate hearts *and* minds, driving engagement and action for your mission.**

These frameworks will teach you the elements of a compelling story, giving you structures and tools to tell stories that will inspire your audiences. Storytelling is a skill like any other. Some people may come to it more naturally than others, just as some people come to tennis or cooking more naturally than others. But with the right instruction, guidance, tips, and techniques, almost anyone can learn some basic skills and improve. I may not be a sous chef, but I can certainly follow a good recipe and prepare a delicious meal that accomplishes my goal of feeding my guests or family. The frameworks in this book will provide you with storytelling recipes to accomplish your goal.

> *From Story to Action* is a playbook of easy-to-use, proven storytelling frameworks that will transform your stories into strategic tools to captivate hearts *and* minds, driving engagement and action for your mission.

These frameworks will guide your strategy for deciding if data are needed in your stories and, if so, how to weave data and story together in a compelling way. For those cases when data are needed, you'll learn exactly how to bring data into stories in a manner that compels rather than bores an audience, pulling them in emotionally, even when the logic of data is at the forefront. You'll learn how to captivate audiences as you explain your complex cause through a gripping story.

Perhaps most importantly, these frameworks will provide shortcut references for you and your team to strategize about what types of stories need to be told for different purposes to different audiences, what needs to be included in those stories, and how to make them compelling. By learning and applying these frameworks, you will lead your teams to connect with both the rational and emotional core of your audiences, making your cause impossible to ignore and driving your audiences to *prioritize, remember,* and *act* on your noble mission.

As you and your team enfold these frameworks into your communication efforts, no longer will you be saying things like, *"We are doing something incredible here, but it's complicated. We've got to figure out how to tell our story better if we want action from our audience."* Or *"We have an opportunity to do something impactful here, but our team needs to tell our story better to get the support we need."*

Instead, you will be saying, *"We are doing something incredible here. It's complicated, but the way we tell our story gets our audiences' attention and enables them to see our vision clearly, making them excited to support our cause."*

WHAT YOU WILL LEARN

We'll begin this journey by getting grounded in some **neuroscience research** that lays the foundation for why stories are essential to your advocacy effort and why stories must be designed in specified ways. Each framework and technique is based on what neuroscience tells us about how stories impact the brain. Once you have that grounding, you will learn different types of stories for advocacy and how to know which type you need for what occasion.

You'll then learn the **frameworks that will help you construct and focus your stories**, depending on your specific purpose and audience. These include the **Story Loop**, a memorable, easy-to-use framework for structuring any story, which will help you know what your story must include and what can be eliminated; the **Tree Tale**, a narrowly focused story; and the **Forest Story**, which zooms out to show a broader context and likely includes the use of data.

Once you understand how to craft the basic contents of the story, we'll look at the **tools you need to refine your storytelling craft**. You'll learn evidence-based techniques to make your stories gripping and memorable. You'll gain insight into **connecting the parts of the story,** so the audience is locked in from beginning to end, even if the story is filled with data. You'll then learn ways to **select the channels for delivering your stories** to your target audiences.

You'll also learn how you and your team can create a cohesive system to **collect and organize your stories** for effective strategic deployment. And finally, an **overarching set of storytelling dos and don'ts** will give your team a set of guardrails for moving forward.

YOUR PATH FORWARD

The more ways you and your team have for talking to one another about your storytelling, the more strategic you will be in telling the right stories to the right audiences in a consistently compelling way to drive action from them.

As you and your team read through the pages of this book, ask yourselves the following questions:

- Which of these frameworks and techniques can transform our message into compelling stories that will ignite action from our target audiences?
- How can we use these frameworks and techniques to build a comprehensive storytelling strategy?
- Where can we use these frameworks and techniques to empower others to help tell our stories?

You and your worthy purpose cannot afford *not* to do this work, and the next chapter will take you into the human brain to show you why.

Chapter 2

THE STORY BRAIN

Why Compelling Stories Work When Other Methods Don't

*You'll captivate your friends and family with this
knowledge at your next dinner party. And knowing this
will reprioritize your storytelling.*

I fell in love with storytelling when my two kids were four and six years old. I took them to the Children's Museum of Indianapolis, where we watched a professional storyteller (I never knew such a career existed) narrate the story of *Peter and the Wolf* as a chamber orchestra played behind her. The event, sponsored by Storytelling Arts of Indiana, so impressed me that I signed up to receive their e-newsletter.

A few days later, a newsletter popped up in my email inbox. The letter announced a call for volunteers to tell stories at the bedsides of kids at a local children's hospital. I thought, "I read to my kids all the time — quite dramatically, if I do say so my-self. I could do that." So, I signed up.

At the training, I realized they wanted us to *tell*, not *read*, stories to kids. Well! That upped the ante a bit, but I took the challenge.

For the next two years, I went each month to tell stories at the hospital.

After a while, I began to wonder if this volunteer gig was worth the monthly night away from my family. Often, my sto-rytelling partner Carol and I would visit 10 hospital rooms a night but only tell two stories because the kids were either so sick or so heavily medicated that they weren't up for a story. Or, they were feeling pretty good and had a sibling in the room to distract them. Or, most often, they preferred to watch whatever was on the big black screen strategically located in their direct line of vision from the bed.

I was on the verge of quitting this volunteer program when, one night, my storytelling partner and I walked into the room of a little girl who was about nine years old. She was moaning and holding her abdomen. We weren't sure if she was up for a story. Then we noticed that instead of being at her daughter's side offering comfort, the girl's mother was cleaning up the room, shuffling papers, clothes, and toys. This wasn't because the mother didn't love her daughter; it was because her little girl's pain was the norm for this family.

So, Carol and I decided to give it a try. We picked up a pipe-cleaner butterfly and flower on her tray and played with those a bit. She seemed okay, so we decided to try something simple — the story of *The Three Little Pigs*.

By the time the second pig was building his house of sticks, the little girl's moaning stopped.

We carried on with the tale, bringing in the big, bad wolf who huffed and puffed. Her eyes got bigger and bigger, while the corner of her mouth turned up just a tiny bit. We finished the story with the wolf landing in the pot. Then we picked up the pipe-cleaner flower and butterfly.

Just fifteen seconds after the story ended, her moaning started again.

As Carol and I walked out of the room, I suddenly realized two truths: 1) I must continue volunteering to tell stories at the children's hospital, and 2) something profound happens when humans encounter a story.

What I didn't know then was how our brains are impacted by a compelling story. However, watching that little girl's moaning start and stop put me on a trajectory to understand why and how stories are so powerful, not only for a sick child, but also for adults making substantial decisions.

As it turns out, in the past fifteen years, neuroscientists have unlocked some of the answers both about what happens in the brain when humans encounter a story and what happens in the brain when humans make decisions. In fact, the neuroscience research shows that the two activities of processing a story and making a decision have everything to do with one another, and that's why stories are essential if you want someone to decide to support your noble cause. So, let's start by looking at what happens in the brain when humans are making decisions, including whether to support your cause.

> The two activities of processing a story and making a decision have everything to do with one another, and that's why stories are essential if you want someone to decide to support your noble cause.

THE BRAIN MAKING DECISIONS

Back in 2005, author Granville Toogood wrote that any time we communicate with other humans, we are engaging one of two parts of their minds: the Conscious Mind, which processes information, data, reports, schedules, budgets, and facts, or the Primal Mind, which processes gut reactions, feelings, likes, dislikes, and values.[1]

Toogood argued that to motivate people to act, we must engage both minds, and the way to activate the Primal Mind is through stories.

He was onto something: Humans don't make decisions through rational, logical thinking alone. We simply can't. Our brains don't work that way.

Despite what we may believe about ourselves as logical thinkers, when making decisions, our brains are engaging regions that conduct abstract reasoning, planning, and organization, *as well as* regions that process emotions, engage our memories, and drive our motivations. This means you must engage multiple parts of your audience's brains if you want to motivate them to act on behalf of your noble cause.

> Humans don't make decisions through rational, logical thinking alone. We simply can't. Our brains don't work that way.

We now know this to be true through neuroscience research.

In fact, for years, neuroscientists assumed that most decision-making was a function of primarily one section of the "higher brain," known as the prefrontal cortex, the space where we engage in the executive function of reasoning. However, in the past 15 years, they have discovered that decision-making occurs in *many* parts of the brain that interact with the prefrontal cortex.

In his article "The Neuroscience of Decision Making," Sam Dabir writes, "Decision making is not a solitary function but rather a collaborative effort orchestrated by interconnected neural circuits."[2]

Nerd out with me on this for a few minutes because it's worth even a cursory understanding of three components of the brain that are active during decision-making.[3]

The Front of the Brain

Even the executive functions of the brain — which we might assume use only rational thought — work in partnership with the emotional functions of the brain. When making decisions, humans use *several* parts of the prefrontal cortex, including the dorsolateral prefrontal cortex and the ventromedial prefrontal cortex.

The *dorsolateral prefrontal cortex* is the most recently developed part of the human brain and is responsible for executive functions like abstract reasoning, planning, working memory, and organization.[4] It is truly the "higher brain," as it is the highest cortical region and is active in rational decision-making.[5]

However, the dorsolateral prefrontal cortex doesn't operate in isolation during decision-making. It works in tandem with other parts of the prefrontal cortex, like the *ventromedial cortex,* which is involved in the processing of emotions, rewards, and the social aspects of decision-making, or how a decision might impact others.[6] Additionally, it works in tandem with the *orbitofrontal cortex,* which evaluates risk and reward.

Already, this information tells us that reason *and* emotion play with one another in decision-making.

Deep in the Brain

Other areas of the brain also display a remarkable interplay between reason and emotion, as various regions of the prefrontal cortex involved in decision-making are impacted by the parts of the limbic system and structures that sit deeper in the brain.

The limbic system contains the *amygdala*, which processes emotions like alarm and caution, bringing gut feelings into our decisions; the *hippocampus*, which helps form and recall memories[7] we use to make decisions; and the *nucleus accumbens*, which plays a role in processing aversion, reward, and incentive that motivate our decisions.[8] These three areas of the brain are most strongly related to *motivation* and *emotion*.[9]

In other words, these areas of the limbic system work in tandem with the prefrontal cortex so that emotion and memory are at play alongside abstract rational thought in decision-making.[10]

You're doing great. Hang with me just a bit longer for a few more terms about the brain. There's no quiz (whew!), and there's also no better way to understand why stories are so important for decision-making.

Connectors in the Brain

Not only do rational and emotional processing centers of the brain work together when humans make complex decisions, but the engagement of neurotransmitters further adds to the thinking-feeling interplay.

Neurotransmitters are chemical messengers operating like internet cables. They facilitate communication between the prefrontal cortex and the deeper ventromedial cortex and limbic system.[11] One such chemical messenger is *dopamine*, which drives us to feel rewards that influence behaviors and decisions. This integration of the limbic system and prefrontal cortex through the neurotransmitters is crucial for adaptive decision-making, emotional regulation, and memory.

As Dr. Bianca Sieveritz notes, decision-making involves a complex "cognitive process... carried out by a distributed network across the brain with many different areas of the brain communicating."[12] In other words, multiple parts of the prefrontal cortex communicate with multiple parts of the limbic system deep in the brain. They do this through the communication channels of neurotransmitters, thus integrating reason, emotion, and memory as we make decisions.

This was an admittedly surface-level, quick trip into the brain. However, it supports Toogood's premise that if we want to move people to action, we must activate more than the rational conscious mind. He suggested storytelling could accomplish that, and neuroscience now explains why he was right.

THE BRAIN ENCOUNTERING STORIES

When the human brain encounters a story rather than data alone, two important things happen:

1. Many of the brain's regions that are central to decision-making are engaged.
2. The brain of the story receiver syncs with the brain of the storyteller, creating a synchronicity that impacts the listener's receptivity to the message being conveyed.

When the brain is confronted with data, charts, graphs, tables, or bullet points of information, only parts of the prefrontal cortex and the language centers are activated. Specifically, the Broca's area and the Wernicke's area are engaged by this abstract content. These regions enable us to make meaning of terms like "prefrontal cortex," "limbic system," and "neurotransmitters," but they don't drive us to take any meaningful action.

In contrast, when the human brain encounters a compelling story with characters and action, many *more* parts of the

brain are suddenly engaged in addition to the language centers.
Researchers using fMRIs (functional magnetic resonance imaging) and the study of blood flow have observed brain activity and chemical changes that occur when humans encounter a story.[13]

Specifically, they have seen that stories activate the prefrontal cortex, the sensory cortex, and the motor cortex. And just like the prefrontal cortex, the sensory and motor cortices interact closely with the limbic system. So, the emotional and memory processing in the limbic system is impacted by the motor and sensory cortices and vice versa.

Think back to our telling of *The Three Little Pigs* to the little girl in the hospital. The further we went into the story, the more parts of her brain "lit up." When the big bad wolf came to the home of the pigs, her motor cortex engaged. When we described the sound of the wolf banging on the door, her sensory cortex activated. And when we got to the most suspenseful part of the story, when the wolf climbed up the roof to get into the house, her amygdala went into overdrive. When that happens, information buried in the story becomes more salient and easier to remember.[14] Who among us doesn't remember the story of the three little pigs?

When the brain encounters a story, not only are more of its regions actively engaged, but it also releases neurotransmitters and neurotransmitter-like hormones. For example, when we hear stories, the brain releases excess dopamine, making it easier to remember something with greater accuracy.[15] And when we care about the characters in a story, oxytocin is released. Oxytocin is the hormone that triggers childbirth and lactation in new mothers, and it's also released in fathers as they hold and care for the baby. In essence, oxytocin is nature's way of ensuring that we connect with and care for others.[16]

When we are on the edge of our seats, wondering how things will turn out for the characters we care about, cortisol is released, just as it is when we lose our keys and don't know how we'll get to an important meeting on time. Cortisol makes us hyper-focused, so when we're engrossed in a story, we're rarely thinking about anything else.

So too, when the brain encounters stress from suspense in a story, it releases dopamine, a hormone associated with pleasure and reward, the reward we get for learning how the story ends. Dopamine impacts memory and motivation. So, we're more likely to remember and be motivated by a story.[17]

Additionally, compelling stories unite the minds of storytellers and story receivers in ways that data and facts alone do not.

Neuroscientists have discovered a phenomenon called "neuro coupling" that occurs when humans encounter a story. In other words, the brain activity of the story recipient mimics the brain activity of the storyteller (whether an author, speaker, narrator, or actor).[18] Their language areas, prefrontal cortex, sensory cortices, and limbic systems sync together.[19]

What does all this neuroscience tell you? No matter who your audience is, no matter how much data and evidence you need to share, stories are key to your ability to connect deeply with your audience and impact their decisions to support your mission.

Here's proof in the form of — surprise! — two stories. Both come from my work training leaders in how to tell stories, with and without data, to advocate for their desired objective.

TELLING A STORY TO IMPACT PATIENT HEALTH

While working with a group of physicians who were in a leadership development program, I met a family practice doctor (we'll call her Dr. Suarez) who was troubled by her inability to convince one of her patients (we'll call him Kimo) to stay current on his tetanus vaccine. Dr. Suarez knew all too well the horrific symptoms that come with tetanus: lockjaw and difficulty swallowing, muscle spasms and arching of the back, increased heart rate, and weakness. She also knew all too well how easily tetanus can manifest from the simplest of incidents, like stepping on a nail, exposing an open wound to dirt, or sustaining frostbite.

For at least six years at various appointments, Dr. Suarez had shared these facts about tetanus with Kimo. She told him the importance of the tetanus vaccine, the data about tetanus cases, and the list of symptoms. Despite her impressive data, Kimo refused.

In our storytelling workshop, which was part of the physicians' leadership development program, one of the story examples I shared happened to be a story published in STAT about a six-year-old boy whose family lived on a farm in Oregon.[20] One day, the boy was playing and fell, cutting open his forehead. Instead of seeking professional medical care, the boy's parents (not medical professionals) stitched their son's wound themselves, and within six days, he showed symptoms of tetanus. For weeks, the boy suffered horrific symptoms, was hospitalized for over 40 days, and spent seventeen days in rehab. All of this came at a high financial cost as well as a high physical and emotional cost to the boy.

As Dr. Suarez heard this example and learned the neuroscience research about the impact of stories on the human brain, she suddenly realized that she had only activated the language centers of Kimo's brain. Thus, she hadn't motivated him to take action.

Dr. Suarez happened to have an appointment with Kimo the week following the training. She again brought up the subject of the tetanus vaccine, but this time she shared the story of the little boy.

The next week, I received an email from the director of the physician leadership development program in which he forwarded the following message he'd received from Dr. Suarez.

Hi Pat,

I wanted to give feedback on the storytelling. I used the story about the tetanus shot on one of my patients today. He is notorious for refusing this shot for years, at least six.
   I told him a story, and he got his shot today.

The story made the difference.

It had reached a different part of Kimo's brain, connected with him emotionally, and motivated him to take action.

While storytelling is not a silver bullet, it's critical if we want a fighting chance at impacting people to act on what we know is worthwhile for them and others.

FINDING THE RIGHT STORY TO IMPROVE PATIENT EXPERIENCE

A team of business leaders who oversee a call center for a pharmaceutical company, which we'll call Innovate Pharma, wanted to derive insights from recorded conversations between their customer service agents and patients, caregivers, physicians, and pharmacists. To accomplish this, the team purchased an AI tool through a company called Authenticx, where I work as a data-backed insights storyteller.

The AI instantly gave the Innovate Pharma team data about their call volume, who was calling, the length of their calls, how many callers were experiencing friction, and more. Excited to have so much data at their fingertips, the team went to the chief commercial officer (CCO) and poured out the numbers, showing the CCO how many people were calling, who they were, and how many conversations were tagged as containing evidence of customer friction. To their surprise, the CCO was unimpressed. They hadn't shown him a specific problem, nor had they shown how this investment in AI was going to save the company money, as he had anticipated. In truth, they had activated only the language centers of his brain.

Disappointed in the CCO's response, the team realized they were providing data with no compelling story, so there was no clear problem to motivate the CCO to act upon.

Coincidentally, the team was signed up for an Authenticx-led storytelling certification training. Our training awakened them to the fact that they had data-dumped without telling a story. They learned many of the simple frameworks for sharing data through story, which you'll read about soon. Just hours into the training, they had a newfound shared vocabulary for talking about how to tell their story to the CCO.

The team went back to the data, looking to understand the root cause behind the number of patients experiencing friction. Upon further analysis, they realized their patients were terribly confused about how to obtain financial help to pay for the medication, which was costly. The company had been communicating only to physicians about financial options for patients, but the physicians weren't giving the patients that information, or if they did, it wasn't always accurate. Consequently, patients were delayed in getting on therapy, which came at a price to their health and at a price to Innovate Pharma.

With this clarity of insight, the team knew the problem they needed their story to convey: Patients were delayed in getting onto therapy because they were dependent on their healthcare providers for getting information and direction on how to get financial support to afford the medication. The team also knew their story needed to compel their senior leadership to invest in a campaign to communicate directly with the consumer of the medication rather than physicians. **Convincing senior**

leadership, their legal team, marketing, and field representatives to invest in this significant business process change would require substantial data proving that the delays from providers were driving a negative customer experience. The data would need to illustrate how this difficult patient experience reflected poorly on their brand and ultimately cost them in revenue.

Using the storytelling skills outlined in this book, they shaped the narrative, weaving in the data and the stories of their patients in a way that activated the language centers, the limbic systems, the sensory and motor cortices, and various neurotransmitters of their audiences.

The impact was palpable. In just three months, after telling and re-telling the story and adapting it to different audiences, they successfully convinced the company to invest over a million dollars in a website redesign and campaign to reach patients directly.

Again: The story made the difference.

YOUR PATH FORWARD

Here's what we know:

1. Decision-making involves multiple parts of the brain.
2. Decision-making requires the interplay of emotions and logic.
3. Stories engage more parts of the brain than facts, data, and bullet points of information.
4. Stories engage the same parts of the brain that are central to decision-making.
5. The brains of storytellers and receivers sync in powerful ways.

To be clear, stories are not a silver bullet to getting your audiences to take the action you want. Neuroscientist Robert Sapolsky makes clear in his comprehensive work that human behavior is influenced by hundreds of physiological, chemical, environmental, socio-economic, and cultural variables that a story might not trump.[21] It's also important to note that the goal of using stories for advocacy is not to manipulate our audiences' hormones and brain functions.

That said, given what we know about our brains on stories, if your mission matters and you want people to decide to act on your objective, **you can't afford *not* to tell compelling stories.**

Just as our telling of *The Three Little Pigs* took that little girl away from her pain temporarily, you want that same physiological impact on your audiences. Only that will give you your best shot at persuading them to support your noble cause.

PART II

Frameworks for Compelling Stories

Chapter 3

THE RIGHT STORY

Match Your Story Type to Your Desired Outcome

*You need the right medication for the ailment
you want to heal. And you need the right story for
the support you want from your audience.*

My husband is the King of Analogies. He's also chock full of leadership and management wisdom and often offers his sage advice through those analogies. Among the best in his repertoire is his statement, "You don't email the fire department." Inevitably, upon hearing that statement, his teams laugh and nod. "It's true," they say, knowing he's really telling them, *if you have something urgent to report, pick up the phone and call... no matter what generation you come from.*

If the outcome you desire is to get the fire department to your house ASAP, you call, but if you want to register a complaint with your local fire department, you email. If you have a headache, you take a pain reliever, but if you have an infection, you take an antibiotic. If you want to support a heavy structure, you use a steel beam, but if you want flexibility, you use a suspension cable. If you want to arrive at a destination quickly, you use your GPS; but if you want to explore the territory and enjoy the land, you use a map.

Simple and clear, right? Use the right tool to accomplish your desired outcome. But to do so, you must know your objective and what tools you have available.

When strategizing about the types of stories you and your teams need to tell to advocate for your desired outcome, you need to know exactly what you want from your target audience. The desired outcome and audience will dictate what type of story you need to tell.

Leaders and their teams who are advancing a cause, great or small, can focus their storytelling strategy best if they know which of the following six stories they need to tell. As you read about these six different Story Types, consider how you and your team, depending on your purpose, may need to build a repertoire of multiple Story Types.

SIX STORY TYPES TO ADVANCE YOUR CAUSE

When you read the words "Story Types," you might be thinking of literary genres like a hero's journey, a romance story, or a comedy of errors. While some of those genres may provide a model for you, when you're working to influence audiences to act toward a particular objective, the following six genres are what you need to get started.

Figure 3.1 Six Story Types

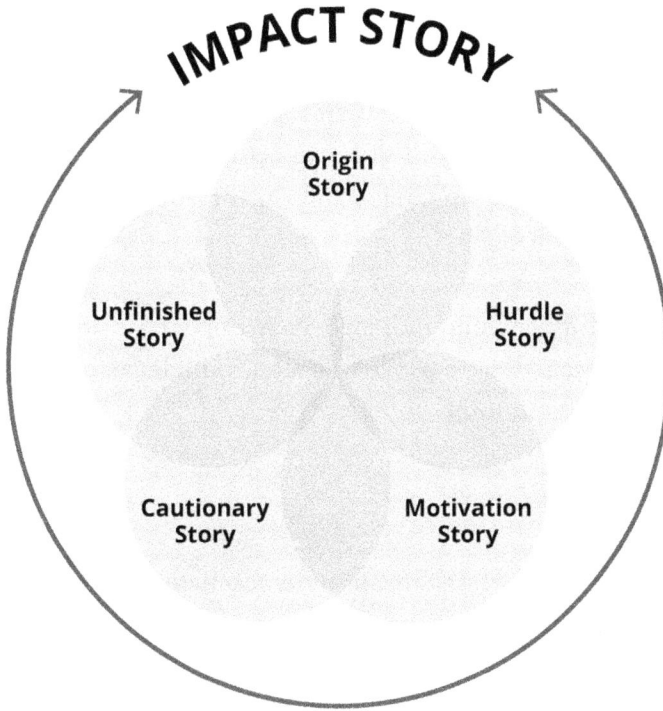

We'll start with the Impact Story, which is at the heart of storytelling for advocacy. The other Story Types are variations on the Impact Story and, as indicated in Figure 6.1, have overlapping characteristics. The value is less in the precise distinction among categories and more in the purpose each Story Type serves.

Impact Stories

No matter what your mission, Impact Stories are critical to proving the impact of the problem you are attempting to solve and the impact of your efforts.

Purpose: Impact Stories demonstrate your initial success in making a difference in order to gain additional support that will grow your impact.

Characteristics: Impact Stories prove the significance of the need or problem you are attempting to solve and, more importantly, offer specifics on the effect of your efforts to date.

Depending on your audience, your Impact Stories might include statistical data to prove impact. (You'll learn how to manage this in Chapter 6.)

Sample Impact Story:

Several years ago, I sat in an audience listening to a presentation from the executive director of a nonprofit organization whose mission is to end youth homelessness in my community. The director shared startling data about the prevalence of youth homelessness in the area, the causes, and the varied needs of these at-risk youth.

Though the numbers escaped me shortly after the presentation, I was compelled to help because of what I did remember — the Impact Story he told. It went as follows.

> The previous year, a set of twin boys, about 11 years old, temporarily lived in the organization's shelter as they awaited permanent housing.
>
> Volunteers noticed that the boys were bright and generally healthy but would decline offers to join in on various activities. At one point, the shelter received free tickets for a large group of the kids to attend an NFL game. The twins

seemed hesitant to go. Knowing the boys liked football, the volunteers gently coaxed them to come along.

During the game, one of the adult sponsors sitting with the boys noticed how bored they seemed. He pointed to something on the scoreboard, but neither twin seemed to look directly at what he was pointing to. Suspicious now, he took off his eyeglasses and handed them to one of the boys, who put them on. In an instant, the boy came to life, enthusiastically responding to everything happening on the field and the scoreboard.

As it turned out, the twins had never had an eye exam and were both plagued with poor vision. The organization culled together funds for eyeglasses, and while not all the boys' problems were solved, their worlds were transformed. The shelter was making an impact, not only by helping youth get to safe and permanent housing but also by meeting basic needs that could transform their lives.

Did I donate to the organization after hearing that story? You'd better believe it. Impact Stories not only demonstrate impact, but they also *have* impact.

Pro Tip on Developing Impact Stories

When developing Impact Stories, you must also consider *which* impact to emphasize.

Different types of Impact Stories will resonate with different audiences. Knowing your audience and your purpose will help you decide what Impact Story is best suited for the context.

For example, universities choose from multiple impacts to convey to different audiences. Prospective students may want to know how the university's internship programs impact graduates' employment rates. On the other hand, when deciding whether to contribute to a new, state-of-the-art science laboratory, potential donors may want to know the impact of the faculty's medical research.

Therefore, to make the greatest impact on your audience and accomplish the chosen outcome, be sure to use the right topic approach.

Impact Stories are a MUST for your advocacy work. Your audiences are unlikely to answer your call without clear demonstration of the impact you are having.

The good news is that you can select from many variations of Impact Stories to use for different strategic purposes.

Origin Stories

One way to prove impact is through your Origin Story.

Whether you, as an individual, have started a small nonprofit to raise funds to cultivate community gardens in your neighborhood, or you work for a large corporation that manufactures safety equipment for large vehicles, somewhere there's an Origin Story that needs to be crafted, documented, and shared.

Purpose: Origin Stories serve three purposes:

1. Helping external audiences understand and align with the motivation and mission — the why — behind your noble work.
2. Preserving the founder's vision and motivation as the organization grows.
3. Lending credibility to the mission, helping audiences see that your motivation transcends personal interests.

Characteristics: Origin Stories recall the germination of the noble cause, taking the audience to the original problem a founder wanted to solve and showing how the organization or efforts evolved to impact the problem.

Sample Origin Story:

In Chapter 1, you read the Empowered Ventures (EV) origin story. Recall that the EV team had two main challenges. They needed to convince select business owners of the value of selling their companies not to an investor or competitor, but to their employees through an Employee Stock Ownership Plan model. EV also needed to convince employees in their newly acquired companies of the financial value to them and the need for them to participate in the business as *owners*.

The EV staff knew that telling their own Origin Story of transforming their family-owned manufacturing business into a thriving, employee-owned company might inspire the prospects to entertain this unconventional option. The Origin Story, they concluded, was an important way for prospects to imagine themselves in a generally unfamiliar scenario. In order to evangelize the idea widely, they needed many of their employee owners to tell the story well.

As you may have experienced, in a young, small company or organization, typically all the members know the Origin Story and toss it about casually over dinners, in meetings, and at small company events. Then the organization grows, and new employees or members are driven by different values and visions. If the Origin Story isn't re-told, the founder's story and motivation for the cause fade into the woodwork.

The leadership team at EV could see the potential dangers of losing their Origin Story as they grew. They knew that if their new staff didn't know the story, they might lack the motivation of the founders and have less success in bringing additional companies into their fold. So, the EV leaders crafted and documented the story so all new employees and new employee-owned companies would be grounded in the shared narrative.

By crafting and codifying its Origin Story, an organization, big or small, can help external audiences connect with the original motivations and intentions of the mission, and it can inspire and unify internal audiences to carry those original motivations and intentions forward as the mission evolves.

Hurdle Stories

Another way to prove impact is through a Hurdle Story.

Purpose: Hurdle Stories may serve one of these purposes:

1. Demonstrating your organization's resilience and ingenuity in overcoming obstacles, thus inspiring support.
2. Restoring credibility in the event of reputational damage.
3. Inspiring a resurgence of support after some decline.

Characteristics: Hurdle Stories show audiences how you or your organization, in advancing your cause, faced some obstacle and turned things around.

Sample Hurdle Story:

Take, for example, this story from the Indianapolis Children's Choir (ICC).

> Over the course of 30 years, the Indianapolis Children's Choir grew from a single choir of 30 kids to a large music organization serving over 2,500 children. The leadership has always known that the organization's impact is not just in training young singers but, more importantly, is in providing a physically and emotionally safe environment for children to build self-confidence, develop friendships, experience diversity, and have a place to "fit in."
>
> So, when the COVID-19 pandemic hit, the ICC, like many arts organizations, was at a loss. The leaders knew they needed to keep their kids singing and socially connected, not just to sustain the organization, but also for the psychological well-being of those kids who depend on the choir as their primary social outlet. They desperately needed to make music together during this time of isolation. But how could the leaders teach *children* choral music without being in their physical presence?
>
> Determined to solve the problem, each week throughout the height of the pandemic, the leaders sent the kids recordings of their vocal parts to learn at home, and each week, the kids sent in a recording of themselves singing the parts.

Then they met together on Zoom for the social connection. When adults began to worry about stalkers on Zoom, they weren't sure what to do.

Then one day, a parent introduced the leaders to employees at Cisco and Webex. They began working with engineers, who built a secure software that would allow the kids to sing and hear one another simultaneously online with no risk of invasion from stalkers. As the engineers built the tool, the choral leaders gave feedback to help the team make technological improvements.

Within a few months, in partnership with Webex, the ICC became the first choir ever to perform a live virtual choir concert. Children from across the U.S. participated, with multiple faces onscreen, each child dressed in their performance attire as they sang complex harmonies and beautiful songs to a virtual audience. In this way, they overcame the limits of social distancing required during the pandemic.

Donors hearing ICC's Hurdle Story were inspired to keep the organization alive. In fact, contributions poured in. In contrast to many choirs that folded during the pandemic, the ICC thrived and came out *ahead* financially because their story convinced their supporters that they could overcome.

Hurdle Stories are a potent tool for building (or rebuilding) credibility.

Motivation Stories

You have no doubt heard a powerful motivational speaker tell Impact Stories, but their focus typically emphasizes individual behavioral change for one's own personal development. These Impact Stories are Motivation Stories, designed to spark a collective effort or an individual action that will benefit individuals or an organization outside of oneself.

Purpose: Motivation Stories seek to influence in these ways:

1. Inspiring audiences to change individual behaviors.
2. Persuading audiences to shift attitudes, values, beliefs, or perspectives.

Characteristics: Motivation Stories are typically personal, focusing on personal behaviors or habits, or focusing on internal states of mind like perspectives on life, careers, relationships, leadership, and more.

Sample Motivation Story:

> I once sat in a full-day leadership retreat that was packed with professional development activities, problem-solving and brainstorming activities, along with announcements from senior leadership about the vision and focus for the coming year, and a host of other changes that managers needed to be aware of. While the day was well executed and productive, I remember only one presentation, which still impacts me to this day.
>
> The COO of the organization — we'll call him Kurt — had the less-than-pleasant task of motivating all company managers to keep a lid on many of the announcements that were made by senior leadership at the retreat. For Kurt, it no doubt felt like a parental moment, needing to tell

the kids, "Hey, you're now privy to a lot of family secrets. Tell 'em to your cousins, and you'll be in serious trouble."

But Kurt was clever. He didn't use the parental finger-wagging approach. Instead, he told a story about a time he and his high-school-aged daughter (both competitive swimmers) participated in an open water 5K swim on a lake. The course simply entailed swimming from one side of the lake to the other, then back again, with each half taking approximately 45 minutes.

As the lead swimmer, Kurt's role was to look ahead every 10 strokes to keep his eye on their target and guide the other swimmers. Because his vision isn't great, all he really knew was that the target was something white on the shore. Every 10 strokes or so, he'd focus on the "something white," keeping the group together, moving in the right direction.

As he swam closer and closer to the target on the shore, he suddenly realized what it was — a very dead body in white underwear. Then his daughter caught up to him, saw the dead body... and freaked out. Within minutes, all the swimmers, still in the water, saw the shocking and disturbing sight.

Knowing there was nothing they could do if they got out of the water, and knowing they had a 45-minute swim back, Kurt told his daughter, whose mouth was hanging open, "just keep your mouth closed, put your head down, and do the work of getting back to shore."

She did. As did the others.

When they arrived back, they called the police. Then the swimmers all agreed it was best for Kurt and his daughter not to tell her mom about what they saw. Again, he said, "Keep your mouth shut."

Within no time, we in the audience understood his point. The company needed us to focus on our work and keep our mouths shut about what we'd learned that day. I'll never forget it.

Whenever I'm faced with an opportunity to say more than perhaps I should, I think of that dead body on the shore and think to myself, "Keep your mouth shut," all because of the COO's story.

To be sure, behavior modification and mindset shifts require far more than being influenced by a single story.[22] But Motivation Stories can help inspire your audiences to examine their behaviors and act appropriately when circumstances might tempt them otherwise.

Cautionary Stories

I'm often asked, "What if my story doesn't have a happy ending? Can that be used to influence people?" Often, the answer to that question is yes — through a Cautionary Story.

Purpose: Cautionary Stories are intended to motivate an audience to take a particular action by warning them of the potential negative outcomes of inaction, flawed decisions, or wrong action.

Characteristics: Cautionary Stories follow the Story Loop, but the characters don't experience an ideal Intervention, so the New Normal is neither a positive nor desirable change.

Sample Cautionary Story:

Recall Dr. Suarez, who needed to convince her patient, Kimo, to get a tetanus vaccination. The story that finally persuaded him to get the shot was a Cautionary Story about that six-year-old boy who wasn't vaccinated against tetanus. From the cut on his forehead and his parents' decision to insert sutures themselves, he experienced months of unnecessary, horrific, life-threatening tetanus symptoms that cost nearly a million dollars.

As the story unfolds, the audience comes to feel sympathetic toward the suffering child and, more likely than not, assumes that by the end, the parents would have jumped at the chance to vaccinate their son against tetanus. But they didn't. Although the boy lives, thank goodness, it's not an especially happy ending. It is, however, a strong caution against the refusal to be vaccinated against tetanus.

Pro Tip for Cautionary Stories

A word of caution around Cautionary Stories: These stories can be powerful tools to drive action largely because they lean into the emotion of fear. While fear is a legitimate and valuable motivator for action, such as preventing us from touching hot stoves, it may not be the most appropriate motivator for the cause you are advancing.

A donor is unlikely to offer a large sum of money to a capital campaign for a science lab because of fear. A team of employees is unlikely to feel positively motivated to comply with a new company policy because they're afraid of punishment.

So, know your desired end outcome and audience when deciding to use a Cautionary Story.

Cautionary Stories should be used with great care, but sometimes they are the very stories that can change an audience's mind and decisions.

Unfinished Stories

Perhaps one of the most important decisions you must make in selecting a Story Type is whether to tell a story that is Finished or Unfinished. In fact, Unfinished Stories are often exactly what's needed when leaders are advocating for change.

Purpose: Unfinished Stories engage the audience in devising or acting upon the Intervention that will help bring the desired outcome.

> Perhaps one of the most important decisions you must make in selecting a Story Type is whether to tell a story that is Finished or Unfinished.

Characteristics: An Unfinished Story establishes the Normal and Uh-Oh (more on that soon). Then, the Intervention of an Unfinished Story is proposed, requiring the audience to act. It is a story in progress.

In contrast, Origin Stories, Impact Stories, Hurdle Stories, Motivation Stories, and Cautionary Stories are finished because, from beginning to end, they describe what happened in the past.

Sample Unfinished Story:

Imagine, for example, that the Indianapolis Children's Choir story wasn't being told as a Hurdle Story *after* they'd managed to work through the challenges of the pandemic, but was being told *during* the pandemic. Imagine that the organization had just discovered the required technologies to sing together virtually, but they were out of budget. The choral leadership would have had to approach their best donors to request a one-time gift to pay for the equipment.

Knowing their audiences might be reluctant to give money for what could be a very short-term investment (How long would this expensive equipment really be needed? What if things went back to normal within a few months?), the leaders might have told a story of the negative impact of the pandemic on the children and the organization. Then, the leaders would ask the donors to participate in the solution so that, months or years later, they could look back and tell the finished Hurdle Story: "Thanks to the generosity of the donors, the children's voices and the organization were saved during those bleak days." The Unfinished Story engages the audience to play a part in the narrative.

I've seen great relief on the faces of leaders as they learn about Unfinished Stories — an option they hadn't considered. "Oh!" they say, surprised. "You mean I can still tell a story even though we haven't completed our mission yet? That's great!"

Key to the success of an Unfinished Story is clarifying what a happy ending would look like and what, specifically, your audience's role is in the story to obtain the desired ending. In fact, you may present the opportunity for your audience to become the heroes of your Unfinished Story.

Better yet, your story may give the audience the opportunity to support the true heroes of your Unfinished Story: those people whose lives your mission will impact.

YOUR PATH FORWARD

The clearer you are about who your audience is and what you want from them, the easier it is to know which Story Type is most likely to help you achieve your objective.

As you've been reading about these Story Types, you may have been thinking, "Hmm, it seems like an Origin Story could also be an Impact Story." Or "Couldn't a Hurdle Story also be a sort of Motivational Story?"

Yes! These genres have overlapping characteristics, and it may be strategic to merge two or more types into a single story.

So instead of deliberating over questions like, "Am I telling an Unfinished Cautionary Story?" or "Is this an Unfinished Motivational Story?" try taking these steps when selecting your Story Type:

- Clarify who your **audience** is.
- Clarify your **desired outcome.**
- Study the different Story Types, asking yourself **which type is most likely to be effective** in your situation.
- Ask yourself **which Story Type will most likely resonate** with your audience.

Simply put, make sure you're using the right tool for the job. Remember, you wouldn't email the fire department.

Chapter 4

THE STORY LOOP

A Fool-Proof Structure for Your Stories

Who doesn't know what a story is? Turns out, many of us.
Yet knowing makes all the difference.

Humans are storytelling creatures. We've heard stories all our lives, and we've told stories all our lives. You would think that means we all know a story when we hear one.

Yet, when people need to tell stories for persuasive purposes, the idea of what constitutes a story often gets fuzzy. My clients share messages that they have identified as stories, but the messages lack the intrigue, focus, and specificity required to create a true story.

In other words, the messages aren't, in fact, stories.

The best way to understand what *is* a story is by starting with a view of what is *not* a story. From there, you can easily understand, appreciate, and use a story structure that will ensure you are telling stories with intrigue.

Consider this example: A few years ago, I was poking around on a website for the Omni Amelia Island Resort, a large ocean resort that hosts professional conferences. As one would expect, the site featured comments and reviews from former guests. Two stood out to me.[23]

The first said this:

> *The entire Omni Amelia Island staff was extremely accommodating and went out of their way to ensure we had a great event. Omni Amelia Island has demonstrated that they are willing to help us create value for our clients, leading to our mutual success. We look forward to partnering with the Omni Amelia Island for future events.*
>
> *— Michelle, Conference Event Manager*

Nice compliment to the resort, right? Exactly what you'd want a guest to say.

Then, I read this review:

> *Michael, one of the service captains, was informed by Rosa (who helped set out the food for our meeting) that I had mentioned to my group that I'd forgotten (or lost) my belt. Next thing you know, Michael brought me a belt that had been left by another guest months ago. It fit perfectly. When I later tried to show my appreciation with a gratuity, he (politely) refused.*
>
> *What none of your folks knew was that I am the president of my group, and so they weren't treating me any differently than anyone else. They genuinely seem to enjoy their jobs and helping people. I have told numerous people about my experiences there.*
>
> *— Joseph, corporate guest*

The difference was striking — and it illustrates the difference between what a story is and is not.

WHAT A STORY IS NOT

In the preceding examples, the first review was a **testimonial**. It makes complimentary statements about the resort, but they are all abstractions. The phrase "They are willing to help us create value for our clients" contains verbs, pronouns, and nouns that are conceptual. In contrast, the second review is concrete and vivid — a story. We can see Rosa, Michael, the food, and the belt. We can hear the refusal to accept the gratuity. We can feel the appreciation and the equity with which the staff treat the guests.

So, a testimonial may be great to share, but it's *not* a story.

Several other presentations of information are also mistaken for stories but do not contain the appropriate elements that make up a story.

For example, a **chronology** is not a story. Let's say my husband and I are having dinner on a weeknight. Being the good husband he is, he lovingly asks about my day, so I start recounting my activities. "I had a meeting with the boss. Then I met with my team and explained the org restructure. Then I worked on a story for my presentation tomorrow..." On and on I go in order of the events as they occurred.

Is my husband listening, *really* listening? He's a great guy, but let's be honest. He's probably partially listening at best. And who can blame him?

Let's say, however, that in the middle of my chronological report of my day, I say, "Oh my land, while I was on a Zoom call with my team, explaining the re-org, suddenly one of my direct reports turned her head and screamed like a screech owl. We asked if she was okay, but she didn't reply, so we didn't know if she or someone else was hurt or what was happening. I didn't know what to do. After all, she lives in Texas, and here I am in Indiana..."

What's happening to my husband now? He's 100 percent engaged and listening. Why? Because I shifted out of the chronology and into a story, in which something went wrong.

So, a chronology may be important to share, but it's *not* a story.

Likewise, a **report** — oral or written — of compelling data is not in itself a story. Say, for example, a director of a marketing department comes to the C-Suite with a worthwhile goal of obtaining a 7 percent budget increase to boost sales and reduce risk of burnout for the overworked marketing team. The director presents an armful of strong data on the market trends, the ROI on the company's lead generation efforts, the ROI on direct-to-consumer marketing, and a cost-benefit analysis of the marketing team's expenditures, as well as data pointing to the long hours worked by employees on the team.

The compilation of data unto itself is simply a **report**, even though it might seem like a story in the mind of the director. And data, like testimonials and chronologies, are abstractions. Compiling the data in a logical order may clearly point to the conclusion that the department needs more funds, but it doesn't put the audience in story mode.

So, a report may contain information that's critical to share, but it's *not* a story.

For influencing your audience — whether presenting a proposal to the C-Suite for an important company policy change, pitching a legislative change to a government official, or making a fundraising plea to a donor — chronologies, testimonials, and reports are inadequate. Simply spelling out the chronology of your nonprofit's work over the last decade is unlikely to compel anyone to support the cause, financially or otherwise. Offering an abstract testimonial of how a patient's quality of life improved because of a lifestyle change is unlikely to motivate another patient. And presenting data that show how a new practice drove up revenue for a similar organization won't necessarily result in adoption by your organization.

If testimonials, chronologies, and reports have their place but aren't stories, then what is? Four narrative components tell us that we are in story mode rather than testimonial, chronology, or report mode.

HOW TO KNOW YOU HAVE A REAL STORY

You can be sure you're taking your audience into a story rather than a testimonial, chronology, or report mode if your message includes the following four characteristics.

Setting

First, we know we're in story mode when we're placed in a setting of a specific time and place. Most Western fairy tales begin with that well-known phrase, *Once upon a time in a land far away,* which instantly cues the listener that they're listening to a story, although "a time" in "a land" isn't very concrete. However, even a vague setting functions as a setup and a cue to the audience that something is about to happen to someone. In the second Omni Amelia Island Resort review, the writer put us in a setting — the conference room during the food setup for Joseph's meeting.

No matter what story you're telling to advance your cause, the setting must be as concrete and vivid as possible. Where and when are important things happening that you will tell your audience about? Putting your audience in a specific time and place engages their motor and sensory cortices and triggers the flow of cortisol. They know from the setting that "something is about to happen," and they need to pay attention.

Characters

Second, stories must have characters. The story about Omni Amelia Island is more memorable than the testimonial because of the characters: Joseph, a resort guest and the president of his company; Michael, the service captain; and Rosa, a food server. We can see each of them in the conference room getting ready for the company event.

When we talk about a noble cause without bringing in characters, the cause can feel distant to the audience. But when we bring characters in, audiences can relate. Even if you are advocating for people in aggregate — e.g., a large elderly population — you need to feature specific characters as central to the story. If you are advocating for something material, say, a land conservation effort, your audience will know they're in a story if they can feel a human-to-human connection with characters who are impacted by that land.

Object of Desire

Third, the characters must want something, whether that "something" is material, intellectual, relational, emotional, spiritual, or metaphysical.

The story about Joseph, Michael, and Rosa in the conference center at Omni Amelia Island Resort wouldn't be compelling if the writer, Joseph, had just said, "Michael, the service captain, and Rosa, a food server, were so kind and helpful." It was compelling because Joseph wanted something

— in this case, something as simple as a belt. Perhaps he needed the belt to hold his pants up because he recently lost 40 pounds, or perhaps, as company president, he needed to look professional. While we don't know his motivation, we know he had an object of desire that drives the story forward and pulls the audience in. In essence, the object of desire sets a course for a plot.

The characters in your advocacy story must want something. Likely, you know exactly what they want because this *is* your noble work. Maybe your neighbors want to be better prepared for a natural disaster, or your department wants a more efficient and effective software application to do their work. Maybe the people your organization serves want to go to college or stay out of the prison system. Perhaps your patients want to be healthy enough to do outdoor activities with their grandkids.

While the object of desire is likely obvious to you, it may not be clear to your audience. The more clearly you paint that desire for the audience and the more relatable that desire is to them, the more gripping the story. Your story will be more persuasive if it makes clear the common goal shared by not only the characters but also the audience.

Obstacles

Finally, a story is only compelling if the characters must face some obstacle in obtaining what they want. Without obstacles, we're back to a chronology or report.

The obstacles for characters might be complex or quite simple. In Joseph's short tale, his obstacle was simple and made clear in six words: "I'd forgotten (or lost) my belt." Not a major crisis, no significant threats to his business or his credibility as a leader, but clearly, he would have felt better if he were wearing a belt. Unfortunately, he didn't know where it was, nor did he have time to find or replace it.

Likely, the obstacles *your* characters face are much more complex than a lost belt. Perhaps your company has regulatory constraints that pose a barrier to the process change you know would improve your customers' experience. Or maybe socio-economic barriers prevent the individuals your organization serves from accessing the education opportunity you offer. Maybe the patients you're serving face environmental, social, and other obstacles, making it difficult for them to adopt the healthy behaviors you know will improve their lives.

These obstacles become the cornerstone of your story. Your audiences need to understand them to support the plan or mission you are advancing.

In sum, the way to get beyond chronology, testimonial, and reporting mode is to communicate about characters interacting within a specific time and place who want something but face barriers in the effort to obtain it. Simple, right?

Yes.

Still, you might be thinking, *Okay, I know who the characters are and the setting. I even know what they want and their stumbling blocks, but I'm lost figuring out how to put that together.*

For that, you need a simple, easy-to-use structural framework that will become as essential to your stories as the steering wheel is in your car.

THE STORY LOOP

In your high school English class, you no doubt learned a plot structure that looked like Figure 4.1.

Figure 4.1 A Typical Story Diagram [24]

Unless you went on to major in English in college, recalling this model may make you want to close this book right now and spend an hour scrolling on Instagram.

The model has utility, especially for novelists and film-makers. However, those telling stories to gain support for worthy causes will find the Story Loop to be a simpler structural framework. This tool is an adaptation of a narrative model recommended long ago for preachers to use in sermons.[25] While your goal is probably not to preach but to influence, the model has great utility and power for anyone advocating for a worthy cause.[26]

The Story Loop is a visual map to help a storyteller convey the elements of setting, characters, object of desire, and obstacles and then prioritize what is and is not essential to the story. See Figure 4.2.

Figure 4.2 The Story Loop

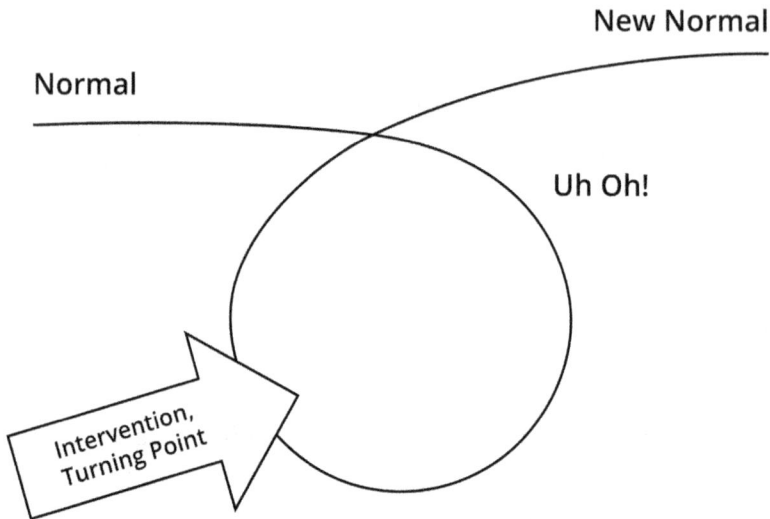

Let's break down the four essential parts of the story in order.

Four Essential Components of the Story Loop

Normal

"Once upon a time, in a land far away, there was a king, a queen, and a princess. Every day, the king, queen, and princess strolled around the pond." Normal! In that statement, we meet some of the characters and have a clear sense of when and where they exist. The audience is grounded in who this story is about and when and where it occurs.

As I work with clients building their stories for advocacy, I notice they often want to jump into the problem, but their audience isn't ready to feel the pain until they have some context. You need to give your audience a few moments to understand who your story is about. Is it about the people impacted by your work? Is it about the staff? Is it about you? The sooner the characters are introduced, the sooner the audience cares about the story because what they really care about are characters for whom they feel sympathy.

The audience also needs clarity about when and where the story is taking place. Without that information, they are distracted at some level, asking themselves: *When was this? Did this really happen? Was this yesterday or a long time ago? Was this here in our office or somewhere else?* These details of time and place ground the audience so they can see what's happening and are then able to go on the journey with you, the storyteller.

Recently, I worked with a group of school nurses who were being trained to use storytelling to help convince parents to keep their children up to date on their measles vaccines. In using the Story Loop, the nurses decided to start their story not with the plea to vaccinate, nor with the problem of kids getting the measles. Instead, they started their story with the school's "normal" before the pandemic of 2020.

"Back in 2019, 100 percent of our first graders here at Roberts Elementary had their measles vaccines."[27] In just one quick sentence, the audience has the context they need. They know when (2019), where (Roberts Elementary), and who (first graders) this story is about. In fact, the audience is primed and ready for the problem to be introduced into the story.

So, use the phrase *Once upon a time in a land far away, there lived a king, a queen, and a princess* as your guide.

Uh-Oh

If the king, queen, and princess just walk around the pond for a long time, the audience will soon check out. Something needs to happen. In fact, something problematic needs to happen.

Audiences who are introduced to characters in a setting during the Normal phase of the story naturally begin to anticipate a phrase like "but then one day," which ushers in a downturn of events. This downturn is an Uh-Oh phase in which something triggers negative outcomes and the associated negative emotions in the characters.

In the case of our nurses, after they state the Normal from 2019, they quickly move into the Uh-Oh, explaining that during the height of the pandemic, between the years 2020–2021, families fell out of the routine of getting annual physicals for their kids. As a result, by 2022, the measles vaccination rate dropped from 100 percent to 77 percent. This decrease led to a measles outbreak that took over 30 first graders out of school for nearly 10 days each, resulting in academic delays.[28]

So, remember the phrase, *But then one day,* to ensure that your story moves from Normal to a pain point on which you can elaborate. Walk your audience through the characters' pain — its causes, the related emotions, and the impact of the Uh-Oh. Make it feel problematic, so the audience becomes hungry for the next phase of the Story Loop.

Intervention

Once your audience has been immersed in the key characters' problem, its implications, and what the characters want or need, the audience is primed to hear the phrase *Along came a fairy godmother who...,* which is the Intervention. This Intervention either has turned things around for the characters or will do so. It may be a policy, a procedure, a program, a technology, an event... whatever has solved, or could solve, the problem. In the Intervention phase, you highlight details of how your cause has made, or will make, a difference.

If you are telling an Origin, Impact, Hurdle, Motivation, or Cautionary Story, the Intervention section will convey what you, your organization, or someone else has done to help resolve the Uh-Oh. For example, in the Omni Amelia Island Resort story, Rosa and Michael intervened in Joseph's missing belt problem, finding a belt that fit him perfectly without his asking and without accepting any gratuity for their efforts.

If, however, you are telling an Unfinished Story, the Intervention section will offer a proposal, an idea, or a recommendation of how to resolve the Uh-Oh. In the case of the school nurses' story, after helping the parent/guardian audience see and feel the pain of the measles outbreak, they outlined a simple plan to turn things around. Their Intervention provided easy steps parents and guardians could take to get their children vaccinated during the summer break.

So, remember the phrase *Along came a fairy godmother* so that your story moves out of the Uh-Oh and into the plan, the program, the solution to help the characters overcome the obstacles preventing them from obtaining what they desire.

If you want to inspire your audience to take specific action, however, you can't end with the Intervention. One more part of the story is needed.

New Normal

Advocates often forget the importance of the final phase in the Story Loop: the New Normal. In a fairy tale, this is where we learn that everyone lives happily ever after, though you might notice that not too much detail is given in showing *how* everyone lives happily ever after. Why? Because the audience would quickly grow bored. In an advocacy story, just enough detail needs to be provided to cast a vision of either how much better things are because of the Intervention or how much better things could be if the Intervention were in place.

In the case of the Omni Amelia Island Resort story, the New Normal is simple, with some implicit and some explicit parts. Implicit is that after Joseph got his belt, he felt relieved, and his conference meetings went on without a hitch. Explicit is his newfound depth of appreciation for the resort staff as he states, "They weren't treating me (president of my group) any differently than anyone else. They genuinely seem to enjoy their jobs and helping people. I have told numerous people about my experiences there." Joseph had a new appreciation *and* was telling others about the resort.

If your advocacy story is Unfinished, the audience needs you to cast a vision of what the New Normal could look like if action is taken. The nurses, for example, decided to cast a vision of getting back to a 100-percent measles vaccination rate. This would ensure better attendance and better academic outcomes for the first graders, leading to greater academic success for those students in their subsequent years of education.

The New Normal vision becomes the critical source of motivation and faith in the ability of the Intervention to turn things around. Keep in mind the phrase *So they all lived happily ever after* as a reminder that your audience needs a vision of how things are or could be better if they act on your mission.

Pro Tip on How to Begin Your Story

Knowing what you want the ending of your story to feature can help clarify how the story should begin. Therefore, decide on the ending before choosing the beginning. Your New Normal will always be a comparison to the Normal to illustrate an achieved or desired improvement.

For instance, if the New Normal shows an impact your organization has had on a community, the Normal needs to showcase something about that community that was the norm at a particular point in time, which will serve as a comparison to show why the New Normal is better.

If you decide the New Normal will be the financial health of your organization, then showcasing the general conditions of the company at a certain point in time may not make sense as the starting point of the Normal, as that won't provide a specific enough point of comparison with the New Normal. Rather, your story might start by telling the audience about the normal financial status of the organization at a certain point in time.

Knowing where you want your story to land will guide where in time it should begin.

YOUR PATH FORWARD

For hundreds of leaders, the Story Loop has worked wonders as an easy-to-use visual guide that transforms messages they *thought* were stories into actual stories.

To ensure you are telling a story and to maximize the Story Loop, take these steps.

- **Examine your message looking for signs that it is not a story:** testimonial, chronology, or report.
- **Ensure your message contains the story elements:** characters in a setting who have an object of desire but face obstacles.
- **Post the Story Loop on your wall, your computer monitor, or some other location** where it can serve as a visual guide to your story construction. (Hmmm... Story Loop tattoo? It's that useful!)
- **Plot your story on a hand-drawn or printed version of the Story Loop** to ensure you are crafting a real story in a strong narrative sequence.

Now that you can envision the structure of your story through the Story Loop, you may be wondering how to scope the story.

Should it be about one person or a single case? Or should it be a bigger story about more people over a longer time frame? In part, the type of story you are telling determines those answers. Two additional frameworks — what I call Tree Tales and Forest Stories — can also guide your scoping. We'll look at those next.

Chapter 5

TREE TALES

A Story Focus That Compels the Heart

*A close-up view of a single tree can illuminate
the value of an ecosystem. A close-up Tree Tale
can illuminate the value of a noble cause.*

My daughter works in the field of environmental conservation and sustainability. Our conversations and the books she has guided me to read over the years have taught me the importance of opening my eyes to study the trees in a forest, or in my backyard, for that matter. Each tree — its roots, its trunk, its branch and leaf structure — nourishes and sustains thousands of life forms, including humans, in its ecosystem.

While I'm not yet even remotely skilled at this practice of observing trees (in fact, I'm woefully bad at it), I have come to understand the power of each tree's contribution to the forest as an interdependent system. From time to time when on a walk in my neighborhood, I sit on a bench and focus on a

300-plus-year-old, 87-foot-tall burr oak tree. I try to observe and imagine all the ways this massive, majestic tree serves other creatures and the earth around it.

On other walks, especially in the fall when the leaves change colors, I focus more broadly on the totality of trees in a forest. When I step back and see the whole, I often reflect on my existence as but a leaf on a tree, alongside millions of other leaves, working our way through the natural cycles of life.

These two different points of focus — one zoomed in on an individual tree and one zoomed out to the broader forest — have much to teach us about strategic storytelling for advocacy. Some advocacy stories need to offer a zoomed-in experience for audiences, while others must offer a zoomed-out experience that allows them to see a broader narrative. This is the difference between Tree Tales and Forest Stories, and both have an important place in advancing your cause.

So, what's the difference and why does it matter? In this chapter, we'll start with the Tree Tale.

WHAT IS A TREE TALE?

A Tree Tale is a story that features particular individuals or groups of people in distinct places where something happens at precise moments in time. In other words, Tree Tales zoom in on a unique case to show a need or to demonstrate impact in an extremely vivid way.

The power of a Tree Tale is its ability to connect the audience emotionally to the lived experiences of specific individuals with whom they can identify. The details in a close-up Tree Tale engage the motor and sensory cortices and stimulate the oxytocin that produces an emotional connection between the audience and the individuals in the story.

Let's say, for example, that I want to recruit weekend volunteers to help prepare meals for families who are staying at the local Ronald McDonald House. The volunteer work means giving up eight hours of a Saturday or Sunday at least once a month to purchase ingredients, prepare a meal at the Ronald McDonald House for up to 75 people, serve the meal, and clean up afterward.

The work is laborious and requires groups of approximately 10 people to conduct the job, so it's not easy to recruit volunteers. After all, people can volunteer for other worthy local nonprofits in the community without having to give up an entire Saturday.

Now, let's assume I have an opportunity to speak to a large company that is asking employees to use their Martin Luther King Jr. holiday to engage in community service. The company has invited several community organizations to talk with the employees in hopes of persuading them to volunteer. Each nonprofit is allotted a few minutes to explain its mission, talk about its community impact, and describe what volunteering with them would entail.

While I would want to give the facts about the Ronald McDonald House and the volunteer requirements, I would also want to share a Tree Tale that would demonstrate the value of the housing and meals to families with children with severe health needs. I could, for example, share this story (with permission from the parents whose names and details have been changed for the sake of anonymity):

A Tree Tale: Misha and Levi

Misha and Levi were small-town island musicians who lived a simple, low-income but joy-filled life entertaining tourists on the Outer Banks of North Carolina.

When Misha and Levi married, they knew they would never have children because Misha once had breast cancer, and the treatments left her unable to conceive. But one day, they encountered a woman on the island who was pregnant, without resources, unable to care for the child she was carrying. As the woman grew acquainted with Misha and Levi, she eventually asked if they would be willing to be the parents of her unborn child. They wholeheartedly agreed.

Soon, they were in an ideal adoption scenario, attending every prenatal appointment, then standing in the birth room as their daughter, whom they named Savannah, was born. Experiencing a dream come true, they brought Savannah home.

But within a few hours, Savannah's skin turned blue, and she was unable to keep any milk down. They rushed her to the hospital. She was sent via helicopter to a children's hospital on the mainland. There, she was eventually diagnosed with Phelan-McDermid Syndrome (PMS), a rare genetic disorder caused by a deletion of part of chromosome 22. The disorder results in not only severe developmental delays, speech deficits, and language deficits but also, in cases like Savannah's, cardiac and renal abnormalities.

The diagnosis led to months and months of costly appointments and treatments requiring them to travel back and forth to the hospital on the mainland, a burden difficult for Misha and Levi to bear both emotionally and financially. Though grateful they had each other, they were also lonely and often bewildered by the debt they were incurring.

They were therefore happy to learn about a Ronald McDonald House on the mainland where, for $15 a night, they could stay together as a family and eat a free home-cooked supper prepared by volunteers.

One night, when Savannah was about three, she was with Misha and Levi in the common area of the Ronald McDonald house for dinner. They went through the serving line to get some lasagna, garlic bread, and salad prepared by the volunteers. Then, they sat at a table with a family who also had a little girl about Savannah's age, also in a wheelchair. Misha and Levi had taught Savannah sign language to help with her speech deficit. At one point, Misha looked over and watched in awe as Savannah signed the word "friend" to the other little girl. The sight took Misha's breath away.

Sadly, Savannah lived only a few months longer, but Misha and Levi remain forever grateful to the Ronald McDonald House, which provided them not just an affordable place to stay during Savannah's treatments, but also a community of families going through similar experiences. They were comforted amid their grief, knowing that Savannah went to her unbearably young grave having made a friend.

My guess is that the employees at the company where I'm recruiting volunteers would give the Ronald McDonald House some serious consideration after hearing this story. At a minimum, the story is so powerful and memorable that if a group of the employees were later deliberating which organization to volunteer for, the Ronald McDonald House would be in the running. It makes clear the meaning and impact the volunteers have, working behind the scenes to not just prepare a meal, but to create space for people in need of community.

The story of Savannah meets our criteria of a Tree Tale because it focuses in on particular characters (Savannah, Misha, and Levi) in distinct locations (Outer Banks, children's hospital of the mainland, and the shared commons of a Ronald McDonald House) at a precise time (when Savannah was born and up until she was three).

Pro Tip on the Story Loop

You may discover that from the beginning to the end of your story, your characters experienced more than one Uh-Oh. In that case, your story may contain more than one loop.

We see in Figure 5.1 that in the story of Misha and Levi, two loops are made.

Figure 5.1 Story Loop Diagram for Misha and Levi

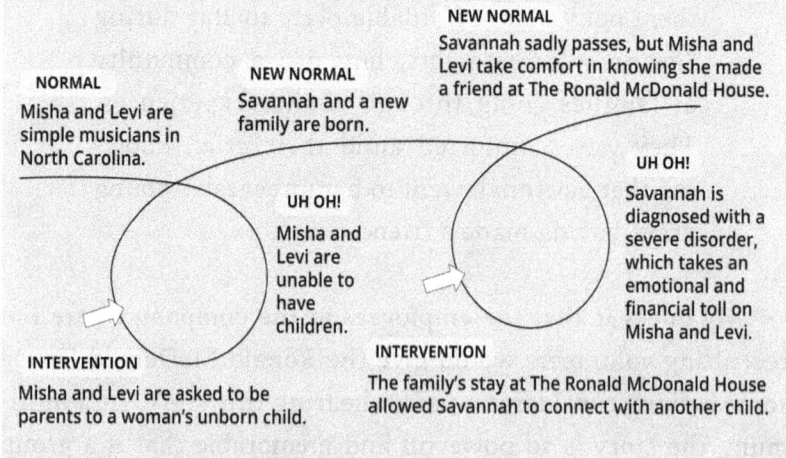

NEW NORMAL
Savannah sadly passes, but Misha and Levi take comfort in knowing she made a friend at The Ronald McDonald House.

NORMAL
Misha and Levi are simple musicians in North Carolina.

NEW NORMAL
Savannah and a new family are born.

UH OH!
Misha and Levi are unable to have children.

UH OH!
Savannah is diagnosed with a severe disorder, which takes an emotional and financial toll on Misha and Levi.

INTERVENTION
Misha and Levi are asked to be parents to a woman's unborn child.

INTERVENTION
The family's stay at The Ronald McDonald House allowed Savannah to connect with another child.

The Tree Tale vividly demonstrates the value of the Ronald McDonald House in a way that the data alone could never convey, making employees in the audience far more likely to consider volunteering for a day of meal prep and service. They can see in their minds' eye the two families sitting together, eating their dinners, and talking, and the two girls in their wheelchairs. The story ignites the audience's sensory and motor cortices, making an imprint on the emotional and memory centers of their brains, which in turn motivates the audience to act.

STRATEGIES FOR A COMPELLING TREE TALE

Here are three recommendations for ensuring that your Tree Tale has impact.

Use Your Landing to Dictate the Setup

For your Tree Tale to be laser-focused without unnecessary details, you need to know where you want it to land. What is the New Normal you want to convey? And what about the Intervention do you want to feature as it relates to your mission?

Misha and Levi could no doubt tell their story of Savannah in many ways for different purposes. For this version, the first New Normal in the first Story Loop was the birth of Savannah and their new family, which is special because of the setup in the Normal where we learn of the couple's inability to conceive, and the Uh-Oh reveals the needs of the pregnant woman on the island. Without that setup, the New Normal would be an ordinary adoption.

The second New Normal emphasizes the impact of the Ronald McDonald House as a financial resource and also a community resource that ultimately helped Misha and Levi in their grief. For the New Normal to land with impact, the Normal needed to set up the reality of their limited financial means as island musicians, and the Uh-Oh needed to highlight the emotional and financial toll of going back and forth to the mainland hospital. Without that setup, the New Normal would be nice but not powerful.

Knowing exactly what you want your New Normal to feature — the *so what* of your story — tells you exactly what details are needed up front in the Normal and Uh-Oh to set the story up for the New Normal to have meaning. When you build your story around the New Normal that you want your audience to understand, your storytelling becomes focused and poignant.

> Knowing exactly what you want your New Normal to feature — the *so what* of your story — tells you exactly what details are needed up front in the Normal and Uh-Oh to set the story up for the New Normal to have meaning.

Provide Context Details to Prevent Distractions

A common pitfall for storytellers is forgetting that what is clear in their minds isn't clear in the minds of their audience. This most commonly happens with story timelines. For instance, while the storyteller can see in their mind's eye how many months or years or days an Uh-Oh lasted, the audience cannot, unless it's made clear by the storyteller. When a timeline is fuzzy, the audience becomes distracted, wondering *When did that happen? Was that before the other thing or after?*

Such distractions from missing details may seem small, but they can cause an audience to lose their emotional connection because they're trying to piece together a timeline in the back of their minds.

Similarly, relevant details about a character's age or demographic might be clear to the storyteller because they knew the individual, saw the individual, or perhaps *were* the individual. Because those details are so familiar to the storyteller, they might not think to mention them while the audience is, again, mildly distracted, wondering, for example, how old a character was when the events of the story happened.

The small details of Misha and Levi living on the Outer Banks and not being wealthy help explain the significance of the commute to and from the hospital on the mainland. The detail of Savannah's age at the Ronald McDonald house clarifies the ongoing treatments and makes sense of her ability to sign the word "friend" to the other child.

Testing a Tree Tale on multiple audiences for their feedback on anything they were missing or wondering about is critical for keeping the target audience *in* the story and emotionally connected.

Don't Rush the Uh-Oh and Intervention

Whether your story is three or 30 minutes, the Uh-Oh and Intervention need to happen at the right pace. To move an audience to support an Intervention, the storyteller must help them feel the pain by providing enough details to convey the emotions that need resolution. Again, it's easy for storytellers to assume the audience can feel the pain the storyteller has felt or seen, but without a statement or two to paint the picture, the audience cannot connect.

Notice how these two simple sentences flesh out Misha's and Levi's pain:

> "The diagnosis led to **months and months of costly** appointments and treatment at the hospital, a **burden difficult** for Misha and Levi to bear not only **emotionally,** but also **financially.** While they were unified as a couple, they were also **lonely** in their parenting experience and often **bewildered** by the debt they were incurring."

The language strategically emphasizes emotions the audience can identify with and produces a need for resolution.

So too, the Intervention needs enough detail that the audience isn't left wondering *how* the Intervention was able or will be able to turn things around. The audience must envision exactly how the Intervention works, especially if you want your audience to support the work of that Intervention.

An abstract statement such as, "The Ronald McDonald House provided an affordable option for Misha and Levi and offered them community with other families in similar situations," would not inspire the audience. What *is* inspiring are the particulars that show how the Ronald McDonald House accomplished those two outcomes. Details like $15 a night, the lasagna meal, common area, the two families eating together, and Savannah signing the word "friend" show how the space, the meal, and the affordability worked to make a profound difference for Misha, Levi, and Savannah.

When you know your landing, provide sufficient context details, and help your audience feel the pain of the Uh-Oh and the relief of the Intervention, your Tree Tale will connect emotionally with your audience and lead them logically to your conclusion.

GUIDELINES FOR GATHERING TREE TALES

When working with advocates who need to tell Tree Tales, I often get questions about how to gather Tree Tales and questions about the ethics and effectiveness of telling someone else's story. For example, can a university gather not just testimonials but also compelling Tree Tales from alumni of a particular program — and if so, how? Is it effective for a charity fundraiser to tell someone else's story? Can a manager ethically tell an employee's story?

The short answer to these is yes. Here are four practices to guide how you gather and tell those stories both strategically and ethically.

Decide Whether to Tell from the First or Third Person

When sharing someone else's story, you must decide whether their story is best told from their voice in the first person, or whether it's best told by a third-person narrator. Consider the following:

First Person — A personal Tree Tale told by an individual holds emotional power. I remember a physician once telling me that he testified before Congress about legislation related to prior authorizations. He was sure he'd told a convincing story about the negative impact on physicians, but then a mother and her wheelchair-bound daughter told their first-person story of how delays with prior authorizations led to the daughter's debilitating seizures. In an instant, the physician could see on the legislators' faces that the first-person Tree Tale was far more potent.

When working with a person offering their story in the first person, collaborate to make sure their story aligns with your goals. It should in some way highlight either the work your organization is doing or the action you need your audience to take.

You'll also need to be sure the individual can shape their story using the Story Loop to maintain focus and using some of the Adhesive and Binding techniques featured in later chapters. The storyteller may need coaching to work within the length boundaries, to ensure the story has the impact they and you are seeking.

Third Person — While a Tree Tale told in the first person is powerful, it's not always possible or desirable. Sometimes the story source is unable or uninterested in telling the story themselves. It may be too emotional for them to tell, or they simply may not feel comfortable as a storyteller. They want to share but prefer that you craft and tell the story on their behalf. Or they may feel that if they tell the story, the focus falls too much on them and too little on the mission you're advancing.

In such cases, it may be best to tell the story in the third person. This gives you control of the Story Loop, ensuring that the Intervention and New Normal both applaud the individual but also convey the need for the audience to help create the Intervention (as in an Unfinished Story) or understand the impact of your cause.

Even when told from the third-person perspective, a vivid story that follows the Story Loop framework and uses Adhesive and Binding techniques will make an emotional connection with your audience. While the Misha and Levi story would no doubt be more potent coming directly from them, if I, as narrator, stay out of the way and let the Story Loop structure and details do the work, the story will have impact.

Use the Story Loop for Interviewing

Whether using first or third person, you and your team may need to conduct interviews to gather Tree Tales. However, interviewing can be tricky. I've conducted story interviews that felt great in the moment of the conversation. Then I began crafting the story and realized I was missing vital details.

A best practice for gathering the right details is to use the Story Loop as a guideline for the interview.

Ask the individuals for specific examples of how their lives were different before (Normal) and after (New Normal) something happened that turned things around. The more clearly you can see the before and after, the clearer your landing will be.

Ask for details about what happened in the Uh-Oh phase and what it felt like — of course, respecting emotional boundaries. If the interviewee is comfortable, ask them to describe as specifically as possible what they feared, worried about, or wondered about in that phase of their experience. Then, ask for details about what specifically helped turn things around in their story. Get as much clarity as possible about how the Intervention occurred.

A good story interview requires flexibility. Most people don't tell their stories in the Story Loop structure when they're talking in an interview. They just talk. Events get described in random order, and memories come out in bits and pieces. An interviewee might talk about their Uh-Oh and their New Normal without talking much about the Intervention. They might jump around in the chronology of events or mention characters you know nothing about.

Ride along on the interviewee's train of thought, but try to place what they're saying in the Story Loop in your mind. As needed, ask them to back up and fill in some details for you. Then, be sure to re-tell the story to them using the Story Loop order to check whether your construction is accurate.

Gather Consent

As you are working with someone to tell their story, you must acquire their consent. Tree Tales belong to the people represented in the story. Unless their story has already been made public and you can credit the source, you must seek the subjects' permission to tell it.

Better yet, invite that person to tell the story themselves in the first person — taking into account the considerations identified above — so they have full control of the narrative. This might mean asking them to tell the story in an audio or video recording you can share with others directly. Or you can use it as a source for a retelling by a narrator. By telling it in their own words, the individual provides language to help the storyteller accurately represent the truth.

In seeking permission to share someone's story, make explicit your purpose in telling it, the intended audiences with whom you will share it, and the delivery channel. For example, someone may be comfortable with you sharing their video recording of the story at a fundraising event but not on social media. Also, seek clarity from the source about any details of the story that they do not want shared or that they want anonymized. The individual or group whose story is being told must be able to trust that it is being handled with care and not manipulated for purposes they do not support.

Represent with Respect

Individuals or groups whose Tree Tale is being told by another must also be able to trust that they are being represented exactly as they wish.

Consider, for example, what character role an individual plays in a story. Perhaps an individual experienced suffering in the Uh-Oh of a story, but they may feel strongly that they were not a victim and do not want to be portrayed as such. Nor do they wish to be stereotyped or profiled.

Avoid representing people as helpless characters desperately in need of your cause. Instead, portray your characters as heroes unto themselves who had the wherewithal to solve their own problems, for which your mission may have been a valuable resource in the journey.

When telling someone else's Tree Tale, ask explicitly how they want to be portrayed as well as how they do *not* want to be portrayed. The narrative must be controlled by the individual, and the more you seek clarification, the more trust you engender.

Seek Approval

If you've ever been interviewed by a journalist, you may know the experience of feeling as though you were crystal clear in the interview and grateful, even, that the journalist was recording the conversation, only to find yourself reading the journalist's article the next day and saying to yourself, "What?? I know I didn't say *that*." This is why, once you've crafted another's Tree Tale, you should seek their approval on it before publishing.

If you're lucky, unlike a reporter, you have time on your side. Use that time wisely to craft the story in your desired format and then circle back to the individual and share it with them. Seek their feedback and final approval. There's no better way to guard against emotional manipulation and exploitation in telling Tree Tales than to garner the full approval of the individuals portrayed.

In seeking their approval, you give the source full permission to add, omit, or correct details. Ask if names or locations should be altered for the sake of anonymity. Ask if direct quotes are acceptable.

When you seek this level of feedback, you demonstrate deep respect for the individuals whose stories you want to tell. You can then feel fully confident in the ethics and truth of your storytelling.

YOUR PATH FORWARD

In making decisions, humans rely not only on the rational functions of the "higher brain" but also on the brain's emotional functions. We engage these through concrete, sensory experience that is memorable and motivating. This engagement requires Tree Tales that zoom into the experiences of particular individuals or groups in distinct places at precise moments in time.

Take these steps to develop Tree Tales to advance your mission:

- **Decide your landing** for your Tree Tale: what you want your audience to know, learn, and decide from the story.
- **Decide the details** to be shared in each part of the Story Loop.
- **Use multiple loops if necessary,** but no more than three.
- **Decide whether the first or third person** should be used to convey the story
- If needed, **interview for a Tree Tale using the Story Loop** to guide your questions.
- **Represent with respect and appropriate anonymity** the people in your Tree Tale.
- **Gather consent** for using another person's Tree Tale.
- **Seek approval** for how you craft another person's Tree Tale.

In the same way that we can see the value of an entire ecosystem by zooming in on a single tree, the value of your noble cause becomes clear to your target audiences when you highlight a compelling Tree Tale. Perhaps more importantly, that zoomed-in perspective creates the emotional connection necessary to drive your audience to act in support of your request.

It's also true, however, that some target audiences cannot make decisions based on a Tree Tale alone. So, you must also know how to tell Forest Stories.

Chapter 6

FOREST STORIES

A Story Focus That Compels the Mind

I always choose the window seat on a plane because the aerial view gives me great perspective. A Forest Story does the same.

Let's face it. No one deliberately chooses the middle seat on an airplane unless they're traveling with a companion. Perhaps you prefer the aisle seat for more leg room and easier access to the restroom. I, on the other hand, always choose the window seat. In fact, it's a sort of spiritual practice because as the plane ascends into the sky and the world below shrinks, my perspective inevitably shifts.

As I gaze at a forest and not just the individual trees, what I had thought was important suddenly becomes less so. The dramas of life seem petty. My very existence becomes small, not meaningless, but small relative to the entire city, landscape, and water masses I see from the air. That shift in viewpoint puts everything into perspective.

Indeed, seeing the big picture from a zoomed-out vantage point is useful, particularly in making substantive, high-impact decisions. When you're advocating for your noble mission, the more you are asking of your audiences, the more they need the big picture that includes the facts and data that support your cause. If you're asking for large sums of money, controversial policy changes, a substantial budget increase, or behavioral changes that are hard to implement, your audiences are not going to act on your request based only on an emotionally compelling Tree Tale. At least, we hope not. After all, making such decisions without information, facts, and data relevant to your purpose would be irresponsible. Therefore, these audiences need your bigger story. We all know those audience members who would hear a Tree Tale and retort, "Show me the data. I just want the facts."

Unfortunately, presenting "the facts" can be challenging. Clients often tell me, "We have all the data, but it's so complicated and hard to explain in a compelling way that we're not able to use it to drive change."

As we saw in Chapter 2, information, facts, and data activate only the language centers of the brain. Our brains shut down at the sight of yet one more graph on yet one more deadly PowerPoint slide. That's why those tactics are less memorable, less inspiring, and less likely to impact a decision, especially when an audience is faced with equally valid data on two sides of a coin.

In addition, while your Tree Tale skeptic is right to want the facts and data, they're fooling themselves in thinking they are Mr. Spock. While no human should make decisions based solely on emotions that arise from a single Tree Tale, no human *can* make decisions entirely from their rational, higher brain, either.

To solve this problem and present compelling big-picture data when a Tree Tale alone won't suffice, we tell a Forest Story.

WHAT IS A FOREST STORY?

Where a Tree Tale zooms in on particular individuals or groups of people in distinct places where something happens at precise moments in time, a Forest Story zooms out to tell a story of people in aggregate over a longer timeframe, in a broader context. A Forest Story still uses the Story Loop, but it does so to present the facts and data in the form of a story. In addition, the best Forest Stories weave in Tree Tales to engage more parts of their audiences' brains.

Let's say, for example, that the senior leaders of a major barge shipping company decide to roll out new safety protocols. All employees, whether they work on the docks, on the barges, or on the 23rd floor of the corporate headquarters, must follow these protocols, which are strict and specific.

Not only will employees be expected to obey the regulations, but they will also be expected to hold one another accountable.

Senior leaders anticipate a battle in getting compliance from over 5,000 employees, especially those who work in corporate offices. So, to introduce the program, they record a video in which the CEO tells a Forest Story that goes something like this.

American Barge Shipping Company: A Forest Story

American Barge Shipping Company was founded 79 years ago in 1946. And for nearly 80 years, we held the track record for having the fewest accidents and the fewest regulatory violations in the industry. That's an *eight-decade* record.

Where our competitors achieved an 83 percent compliance score *at best*, we achieved a 100 percent compliance score year after year after year. Where our competitors experienced, on average, 3 deaths and 42 injuries annually, we experienced, on average, 0 deaths and 6 injuries annually.

In the past decade, however, the widespread use of smartphones and other electronic sources of distraction has put safety at risk for our entire industry. A 2017 study showed that the mere presence of a smart device can cause "brain drain" — diminished function of memory and fluid intelligence.

Simply put, we're not as sharp when we are attached to our phones, which means our safety is at risk. And sadly, we at American Barge were living proof of those distractions this past year. We lost not one, not two, not even three, but *four* of our employees on our barges and docks, bumping us from first to thirteenth place in the industry safety rankings.

Far worse than the drop in our safety rankings is the impact of the loss of these four members of our family.

Jamal worked the graveyard shifts as a deckhand on the docks. One night in June, he was on his phone and took a step backward, fell over a railing from the upper deck of the barge into the freight cars, and broke his neck. He died three days later, leaving behind his wife Jessie and their twin boys, Maj and Zeek.

Louie was a marine mechanic who oversaw the maintenance of all barge and dock mechanics. While rushing to get equipment for a repair job, he rushed down the steps of the mechanic's shop. Arms full of equipment, Louie stumbled down two flights of stairs and died on impact, leaving behind his parents, three sisters, and eight adoring nieces and nephews who called him Uncle Goofy Louie.

Rhonda was a dredging operator who used dredging equipment to clear waterways for the safe passage of barges. She took a call from her supervisor while working near the electrical wiring for the dredging equipment. Distracted by the conversation, she tripped over the wiring and fell into a dredge machine, which took her life. She and her husband had been married for just six months.

Raj was a tankerman who loaded and unloaded liquid cargo. While on a break, he was playing a game on his phone and didn't notice a leak in the cargo. He dropped his cigarette onto the liquid and was instantly engulfed in flames, leaving behind his partner of six years.

We in this company are a family. These were our brothers and sisters who died in these tragic accidents. None of them was doing anything wrong. They were doing exactly what we all do today. Like all of us, they were in the presence of devices that cause "brain drain."

These tragic deaths taught us it's time to update our safety protocols and policies with guidelines that will make us more conscious of our surroundings, our movements, and how we are using our devices. So, we are rolling out a new safety program called "Dare to Care" in which *all* of us, whether we work on the docks, the barges, or in corporate headquarters, will

FROM STORY TO ACTION

follow the same rules that we know will keep safe those in the greatest danger.

We are asking all employees to practice these protocols, including *Never take a step backward. Never talk on one's cell phone while walking. Always hold the handrail while on an escalator or staircase.* More will be shared in writing.

We will *all* follow the rules because we are a family.

Rules work when they apply to every family member and when each family member cares enough to hold one another accountable. So, we are asking each of you not only to follow the rules yourself, but to look out for one another. When you see a co-worker violating a rule, tap them on the shoulder, then quietly and respectfully remind them of the rule for their own safety.

We believe that if we re-train ourselves to be as aware and alert as we were before the days of smartphones, we can not only regain our status as number one in the industry for safety, but more importantly, we can and will avoid losing even one more precious family member.

So, make your commitment with me: Dare to Care, to protect yourself and your brothers and sisters here at American Barge.

The story of American Barge meets our criteria of a Forest Story because it zooms out to the broader context of the company's history and the broader cultural context of living in a smartphone world.

Notice, too, how this story also follows the Story Loop, weaving the data and four Tree Tales into the narrative (see Figure 6.1).

Figure 6.1 American Barge Shipping Story Loop

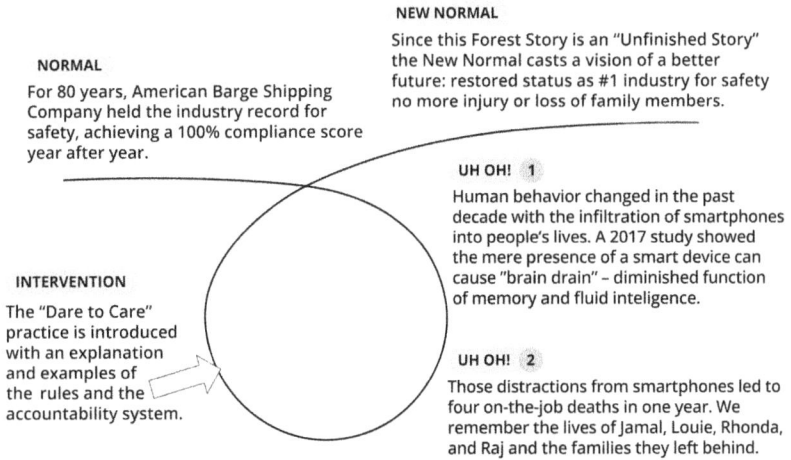

NEW NORMAL

Since this Forest Story is an "Unfinished Story" the New Normal casts a vision of a better future: restored status as #1 industry for safety no more injury or loss of family members.

NORMAL

For 80 years, American Barge Shipping Company held the industry record for safety, achieving a 100% compliance score year after year.

UH OH! 1

Human behavior changed in the past decade with the infiltration of smartphones into people's lives. A 2017 study showed the mere presence of a smart device can cause "brain drain" – diminished function of memory and fluid inteligence.

INTERVENTION

The "Dare to Care" practice is introduced with an explanation and examples of the rules and the accountability system.

UH OH! 2

Those distractions from smartphones led to four on-the-job deaths in one year. We remember the lives of Jamal, Louie, Rhonda, and Raj and the families they left behind.

In this situation, if only the Tree Tales were told, employees who sit safely tucked behind a desk in corporate headquarters might feel sympathetic for the loss of the four employees but remain unconvinced that they, too, need to follow rules that seem irrelevant to their jobs. But by including data, the Forest Story allows those skeptical employees to see themselves as part of the narrative, even if they were not connected to the four accidents. The data are strategically placed in the story to draw in every employee as part of the human experience of brain drain from smartphones and part of the American Barge almost-80-year-old family that values employee safety. The story takes the aggregate character of 5000 employees and makes them family members.

Using the Story Loop structure and making the audience characters in the bigger company historical and cultural narrative, the CEO makes the safety performance data intriguing rather than dull. The structure, even with data, builds suspense (*"The company used to be #1, but then things changed..."*), which triggers the release of cortisol in the audience, resulting in focused attention. And by weaving the Tree Tales into the Forest Story, the CEO humanizes the data, triggering the release of oxytocin, resulting in increased sympathy and a greater chance of changed behavior.

STRATEGIES FOR A COMPELLING FOREST STORY

Want your Forest Story to have high impact? Consider these three recommendations.

Know Your Landing

Just as with Tree Tales, Forest Stories can fall flat without a clear "So what?" So, before you start plotting the details, data, and structure of your story, decide where you want it to land. What's the New Normal you want your audience to see or envision?

Write out your landing in a simple, clear declarative sentence. Then put that landing within sight as you craft the story. Doing so will keep you focused on the right narrative and data details that will lead your audience to your desired conclusion.

Two important questions to ask yourself in deciding where you want your story to land:

Question 1: Is this a Forest Story in which the New Normal has been realized?

If so, before crafting your story, decide what you want your audience to know and feel about the new state of things.

Perhaps you want your audience to see the positive impact your organization has had on children in your community after having implemented a multi-million-dollar, city-wide program two years ago. The New Normal will dictate key data points that you know your audience must hear to understand and appreciate the significance of the New Normal.

Question 2: Is this a Forest Story in which the New Normal has not yet been realized?

If so, your task is to cast a vision, through data, of the ideal state you hope your Intervention will create.

Let's back up and say you are just now proposing the multi-million-dollar citywide program, and you seek funding from a local charitable foundation. The Intervention of your story explains the program, and the New Normal must cast a vision for the impact you anticipate the program will have. Relevant data might show how similar programs in other locations have had an impact, thus presenting a vision of the same impact in your community.

Or you might present the data you *anticipate* will be the result of the program, saying, "If we can get this program off the ground in the next three months, we project that the numbers could change from X to Y."

Knowing whether your New Normal is a current reality or a vision of the future will indicate what data will move your audience to action.

> Knowing whether your New Normal is a current reality or a vision of the future will indicate what data will move your audience to action.

Structure First, Data Second

When my clients need to present data to tell the story, they're inclined to compile all the data they want to share. Unfortunately, they end up in the weeds, convinced that every data point they have is important and their audience needs to hear and see it all. DANGER! This inclination results in data dumping.

Here's how to avoid data dumping: After identifying the New Normal landing, plot your storyline and *then* figure out what data points are needed to support the storyline. Of course, this approach assumes you have already analyzed the data and are basing your story on what you learned in your analysis.

An easy way to plot out your story is to have the Story Loop in front of you. Take these steps:

- Literally, draw the Story Loop, then make notes in each section of the loop.
- Because you've already decided on your landing, make notes of what you want to say about the New Normal, including (if your story is Unfinished) a vision of what the context could look like if the Intervention were implemented.
- Then go to the Normal section, making notes about the context your audience needs to understand. Think setting: time, place, and introduction of characters.
- Then name the Uh-Oh, making notes about what problems or pain points you need the audience to understand and feel.
- Next, list what the audience needs to understand about the Intervention. What specific actions could or did turn things around?

Once you see this structure, *then* go back and identify which data points are necessary in the different parts of the story. Ask yourself if you need a data point to prove what was Normal. Or do you need data to prove the Uh-Oh? Perhaps you need data to prove what the New Normal looks like today. When the story structure is laid out first, you will select only the most relevant, persuasive, and compelling data to include.

Pro-Tip on Data Volume in Forest Stories

To make your data meaningful, make every effort to limit how much of it you include, featuring only that which illustrates the narrative.

For example, to help your audience feel the pain in your Uh-Oh, you might strategically organize just two to five strong data points that show the worsening of a problem and its impact. And be sure to connect those data points with the narrative from your Story Loop to keep the story front and center.

You might state, for example, *"These numbers ultimately mean that the vulnerable children of our community don't have a fighting chance of breaking generational cycles of poverty, addiction, and misery — cycles no one aspires to."* This kind of statement connects the data to the story you're trying to tell without assuming the audience will make the connection on their own.

Consider using limited data in the New Normal to cast a vision in an Unfinished Story. For instance, you might say, *"While so much data proves the success of this program, three statistics are most telling."* You can then elaborate on those three data points and avoid data dumping at the end of your story.

Don't start preparing your story by making PowerPoint slides filled with pretty graphs and charts. Do analyze your data. Then craft your story and let the narrative dictate what data needs to be included.

I even recommend telling your story to someone without reciting any data at all, just to see if the narrative hangs together. You'll be amazed at how much data can be left on the cutting room floor when you're focused on the story structure.

Weave in Tree Tales

Whenever possible, weave a Tree Tale into the story to humanize the data. If you are strategically revealing the data within the context of the story structure, your audience will be locked in, needing to know how the Uh-Oh will get resolved. Heighten the impact by adding in a Tree Tale that connects the audience's rational understanding of the problem to their emotional understanding, as they see the specific human impact the data are pointing to through the experience of particular people at specific points in time.

Tree Tales can be woven into any part of the story. Consider your audience when making a strategic decision about where to insert one. Perhaps you want a Tree Tale early on to captivate your audience and show the relevance of your story to human lives. However, if your audience is data-driven, you may be better off weaving in your Tree Tale *after* you've presented several strong data points. Perhaps you share a Tree Tale in the Intervention or New Normal to illustrate how the solution you're proposing could make a difference.

Think carefully about your audience's receptivity to an integrated Tree Tale, but don't shy away from its power to motivate and inspire action, especially when coupled with convincing data.

Consider Multiple Story Loops

Often, I get asked, "Is it possible to have more than one loop in my Forest Story?" The answer to that is a resounding YES! With, of course, the caveat that you don't want a story with endless loops.

Telling a Forest Story that spans a relatively long period of time will likely require multiple Story Loops. Your Forest Story might look something like Figure 6.2.

Figure 6.2 A Story with Multiple Loops

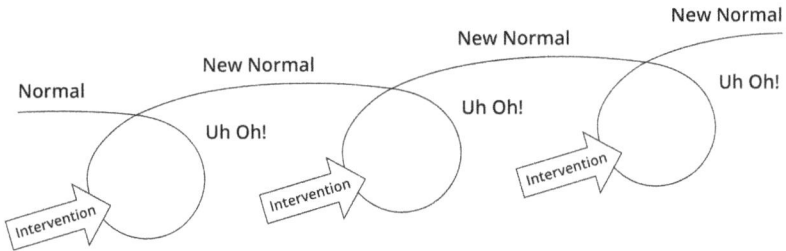

Recall from Chapter 1, the Origin Story that Emily and others at Empowered Ventures needed to tell in order to convince other business owners to sell their companies to their employees. As Emily began crafting the EV Origin Story, she asked, "Can a story have more than one loop? I think more than one Uh-Oh got us where we are." So, she built the story around three Uh-Oh moments, each of which was resolved with an Intervention that got them to a New Normal.

Loop One: A business owner wanted to retire but couldn't find anyone to sell the company to who would maintain the culture he had built there. They put the company into a trust and are selling the shares back to the employees, thus preserving the company culture and stimulating growth and financial success.

Loop Two: Amid the growth and financial success, they recognized the risk in an economic downturn and the need for a diversification safety net. So, they became an employee-owned holding company, buying and converting into ESOP five other companies, all of which experienced substantial growth and employee financial welfare.

Loop Three: In becoming a holding company, they needed a system to help new employee-owned companies thrive. After developing five pillars for success to guide the newly transformed ESOP companies, they now envision a future in which they welcome into the fold 5, 10, 20, 50, 500 more employee-owned companies.

The three loops draw the audience into the struggle and relief, struggle and relief, struggle and relief. But if the story carried on with more than three struggles, the audience would likely begin to feel antsy. So, I recommend no more than three loops in your Forest Story.

YOUR PATH FORWARD

When faced with an audience that (wisely) demands the facts, the numbers, the data, and the broader picture, the Forest Story is your tool. But data dumping doesn't interpret the facts and statistics in a meaningful or persuasive way. The data must be presented within the framework of the Story Loop.

Take these steps if you want to tell a Forest Story to your audience:

- Consider the size of the planned ask.
- Determine whether your audience is likely to be skeptical of a Tree Tale alone.
- Decide the points to be shared in each part of the Story Loop.
- Use multiple loops if necessary — but no more than three.
- Then decide what data are needed to prove each part of the story.
- Add in Tree Tales where needed to connect more deeply with your audience's emotions.

The Story Loop structure can transform a dull presentation chock-full of data slides into a compelling narrative, presenting relevant data at just the right moment to keep the audience wanting to know what's coming next.

For many audiences, the Forest Story framework provides the aerial view that gives audiences the perspective they need to enact change.

PART III

Techniques for Great Telling

Chapter 7

ADHESIVES

Tools to Make Your Stories Stick

Resin is a thick, sticky fluid that preserves a tree for years.
For your message to be lasting, you need story resin.

Whether you're telling a Tree Tale or a Forest Story, if you want
your audience to remember and be energized by your story, if
you want your stories to be so compelling that people say, "I just
can't shake that story; I've got to do something," then you need
Adhesives — techniques that will make your stories stick.

I first learned about resin when my son played violin. He would
apply rosin — derived from tree resin — to his bow. The sticky resin in
rosin gives the bow the grip it needs to glide easily across the strings
and extract beautiful sounds. The sticky, adhesive quality matters.

In fact, resin's sticky quality seals and protects a tree, helping it endure for years.

So too, you want that sticky quality in your story so that it will
endure in the minds of your audience. And now that neuroscientists have discovered how stories work in the human brain, we
know which storytelling techniques stick in the brain to impact
decision-making.

Because these brain functions are central to human decision-making and because you want your audiences to act on your behalf, once you have decided your story's content using the Story Loop, Tree Tale, and Forest Story frameworks, you need to incorporate five techniques in the *telling* of your stories to engage as much of the brain as possible. These are the adhesives that will cause your stories to stick with your audiences.

ESSENTIAL ADHESIVE TECHNIQUES

Vivid and Identifiable Characters

I'll never forget one of my favorite professors saying, "It's always better to talk about *a person* than to talk about *people*." In other words, audiences are more captivated when you talk about a specific person than when you speak in generalities about *people*. Specific characters are how we relate to a story and get locked in.

In neuro-economist Paul Zak's famous work on why inspiring stories make us react, he and his colleagues created a short, animated video of a father at the park with his two-year-old, bald son, Ben, who has terminal brain cancer. The father speaks of his struggle to enjoy and play with his son, knowing his son only has a few months to live. But eventually, the father decides he must stay emotionally close to his son through to his last breath.

Zak and his colleagues tested their subjects' blood both before and after they saw the video. Tests revealed significant increases in oxytocin levels after encountering the story. In fact, oxytocin levels were higher among the subjects who saw the video than those who saw a different video without the details about the father and son. Why? Because the audience who got the details were compelled to care about Ben and his father. Zak concluded that "To the brain, good stories are good stories, whether first-person or third-person, happy or sad, as long as they get us to care about their characters."[29]

To care about the characters, your audience must see them in their mind's eye, so the characters need to be **vivid.** One way to make your characters vivid in a Tree Tale with just a few words is by *giving them names.* If you need to, change the name for anonymity by saying, for example, "a boy, we'll call him Ben."

You can also make a character vivid by ascribing one or two *vivid characteristics* to them, something as simple as "a two-year-old son with no hair because of his chemo treatments." We can see that little boy Ben's bald head as he plays in the park. Suddenly, our sensory cortex lights up, and we're connected.

Not only do the characters need to be visible, but they also need to be **identifiable.** You can accomplish this task by helping your audience relate to what the characters *feel.* The characters in *The Wizard of Oz* are memorable because they're so vivid, but we also love them because they're identifiable. I have no idea what it's like to be a Scarecrow, but I certainly know what it's like to want to be smarter than I am. I don't know what it's like to be a Tin Man or a Lion, but I know what it's like to want love and courage. We identify with what the characters feel.

So, let your audience in on the emotions of your main characters. The story of Ben and his father was simple, short, and animated, but the audience cared about the two by learning how the father struggled to connect and play with his son, whose death was imminent. Even without having gone through the same experience, audiences can identify with the father's fear that connecting with Ben might increase his pain upon his son's passing.

Because Ben and his father were vivid and identifiable, the subjects in the experiment experienced elevated levels of oxytocin. More importantly, when given the opportunity to donate after the experiment, the subjects who encountered the story of Ben donated *five times as much money* to the cause as those subjects who didn't get the story.[30]

Pro Tips on Forest Story Characters

As you would with a Tree Tale, in telling a Forest Story with data, you need to make your aggregate characters vivid and identifiable by giving them characteristics and emphasizing their feelings.

Recall the Forest Story in Chapter 6 about American Barge Company, which lost four employees through preventable accidents. The story referred to the employees (broad category) as "our family members" (more vivid and identifiable). Suddenly, the data point about the decline of their safety score has been humanized, and it now carries emotional weight.

An even better way to make aggregate characters in Forest Stories vivid and identifiable is by strategically weaving in Tree Tales, as the barge company CEO did.

Let's look again at the Innovate Pharma example from Chapter 2. Upon analyzing the data, their patient services team realized patients were encountering financial issues in obtaining their medication. Their stories used quantitative data to show senior leaders the prevalence of the complications, thereby providing the broad context. And upon hearing and seeing the prevalence data, the senior leaders generally paid attention. However, when the team also wove patients' audio voice montages through the story as Tree Tales, depicting the situations of individual patients and their caregivers in their own words, the magic happened.

The moment the company leaders heard the voices of patients saying things like, "Why is getting insurance to pay for this medication so complicated?" "I simply can't afford this," and "My doctor never explained this process to me," they immediately felt sympathy toward the real people represented by the quantitative data. Inevitably, the leaders shifted into problem-solving mode because they'd come to care about the characters, whose plight they now saw much more intimately.

When your stories contain vivid and identifiable characters, your audience will connect not just with the characters but also with you and your worthy cause. Paul Jenkins writes that "characters are the heart of a narrative and need to be developed and relatable to cultivate connection" with the audience. In fact, the more the audience relates, the more they experience neuro-coupling with the storyteller; i.e., their brains sync with the brain of the storyteller.[31]

You want your audiences to sync with you around your worthy mission.

Suspense

Ever wonder why you get sleepy during a lecture or presentation, even though you had a good night's sleep, but you're wide awake while watching a psychological thriller late at night, though you're running on four hours of sleep? It's all in the suspense.

Suspense and surprise cause the release of dopamine, which, as we learned in Chapter 2, rewards our brains and encourages us to continue paying attention as we anticipate the resolution in the story.[32] When dopamine is activated, your story is more likely to be remembered.

Paul Zak and his team observed that their research subjects had elevated levels of cortisol in their blood after hearing the story of Ben and his father. Remember? Cortisol is a stress hormone our brain releases when we encounter suspense. When we need to know what's coming next in a story and how the characters' problem will get resolved, the release of cortisol causes us to focus our attention.

The suspense in your story doesn't need to be at the level of a horror film. In fact, the Story Loop framework automatically builds suspense. When you start with Normal, introducing characters in a setting, the audience may be more or less pulled in if the characters are vivid and identifiable. But the Uh-Oh of the story is the moment when the suspense kicks in. Something goes awry, and the audience needs to know how it will get worked out for the characters. In fact, the more the audience feels the characters' pain, the more invested they are in needing to know the resolution.

Again, you may be asking, *can a Forest Story with facts and data contain suspense?* Should it contain suspense?

Yes, but it must be done with care.

Just as with a Tree Tale, a Forest Story should be structured using the Story Loop, which will automatically generate suspense. For example, when telling the stories of their patients struggling to afford their medication, the Innovate Pharma storytellers started the story with data that established the Normal: the total volume of conversations they'd analyzed, the percentage of conversations with patients vs. caregivers vs. doctors' offices, and so on. Then, they moved into the Uh-Oh by providing data that showed how many patients were talking about the need for financial support. With data as proof, suspense built as the storytellers warned, "Worse yet, the patients talking about financial support are also expressing high levels of confusion because they'd received misinformation from their physicians."

With this suspense, the audience naturally asked, *"What's the confusion about?"* Then, when the storytellers shifted into a few Tree Tales of voices from the patients, the suspense was greater still as the audience listened and needed to know what would happen for those patients. At this point, the audience was asking, *"What are we doing to contribute to the confusion? How can we fix this for patients?"*

In many stories, the Intervention and New Normal relieve the suspense for the audience, inspiring them to support a cause because they've seen the impact of the noble mission. But in an Unfinished Story, the audience may leave the story still in a state of suspense, which can motivate them to get relief by taking action.

You see, suspense is not only a way to capture attention but also a way to drive a response from your audience.

Two words of caution about your audience and suspense:

1. Consider the audience in deciding how much suspense to build into a Forest Story.

    Often, executive-level audiences want to know the *so what* or the bottom line of a story and have little tolerance for suspense. In that case, it may be necessary to state the New Normal in the form of an executive summary up front to satisfy that audience's need. Then, you can walk the executive through the story of how you reached the conclusion. Once in the story, you can still use suspense.

2. If the suspense goes on too long, your audience will lose interest.

    The Uh-Oh of the story must build enough suspense to create a need for resolution, but there's a limit to the amount of suspense an audience will tolerate. A reader who has selected an 800-page novel may be willing to sit in suspense for days, but the audience of a story for your mission won't have that kind of patience.

Concrete, Sensory Images

Many years ago, I heard a Tree Tale from someone raising funds for a local charity. Her main character was a little girl, six years old, who came every day to an after-school program for families in need. The storyteller described the little girl as always wearing the same polka-dot dress. In fact, the fundraiser mentioned the polka-dot dress three times in the story, and I still remember it today. It was a sticky detail.

Concrete sensory images like a polka-dot dress can be conveyed with just a few words to help your audience see, feel, hear, taste, or smell something specific in their minds. Whether you use descriptive words, visual images in the form of videos and photos, or the auditory sounds of voices, these images will activate your audience's sensory and motor cortices, engaging the memory and emotion functions of their brains.

How do you incorporate concrete, sensory images into a Forest Story? Again, by weaving Tree Tales into Forest Stories.

Let's revisit our hypothetical Forest Story from Chapter 6 about the American Barge Shipping Company. The story began with data about when the company was founded and the number of years it held the industry record for the fewest accidents and fewest regulatory violations. Then, the story offered more data, revealing the increase in accidents, injuries, and deaths caused by smartphone distractions.

> "Where our competitors achieved an 83 percent compliance score *at best*, we achieved a 100 percent compliance score year after year after year. Where our competitors experienced, on average, 3 deaths and 42 injuries annually, we experienced, on average, 0 deaths and 6 injuries annually.
>
> In the past decade, however, the widespread use of smartphones and other electronic sources of distraction has put safety at risk for our entire industry. A 2017 study showed that the mere presence of a smart device can cause 'brain drain' — weakening our memories and fluid intelligence.
>
> And sadly, we were living proof of those distractions as this past year as we lost four of our employees on our barges and docks, bumping us from first to thirteenth place in the industry safety rankings."

The data alone are compelling, but our sensory and motor cortices aren't engaged until the Tree Tales of the individuals who died come into the Forest Story. When we suddenly hear the vivid details that Jamal (named character) was on his *phone* and took a *step backwards*, fell over a *railing from the upper deck of the barge into the freight cars*, and that Louie *rushed down the steps* of the mechanic's shop, *arms full of equipment* when *he stumbled down two flights of stairs*, our brains are more engaged, we "sync" with the storyteller, and the story becomes unforgettable.

Whether telling Tree Tales or Forest Stories, you need to activate the many areas of your audience's brains that are essential for decision-making. Just a few simple, concrete, sensory details can accomplish this.

Showing vs. Telling

Perhaps, you, like me, have uttered these words: "I didn't really know how bad the situation was until I saw it for myself." We all say that from time to time because no matter what people *tell* us, sometimes we just don't get it until we see it.

Showing makes the feelings of your characters identifiable to audiences far more impactfully than does *telling* audiences how your character felt. After all, feeling words are abstractions. When you say, "she felt scared," "they felt worried," "he was confused," you're telling the feeling, leaving your audience disconnected.

But audiences engage when they see the feelings at play. It's one thing to say, *"the boy got tetanus and was miserable,"* but it's an entirely different thing to say, *"the boy's back arched as his muscles spasmed any time light came into the room or when his parents and doctors spoke aloud in his presence."* The first statement tells us he was ill. The second statement shows us not only that he was ill but also how he felt without ever saying "he was miserable."

Because Tree Tales feature people at specific points in time, your audience needs to know how those individuals feel throughout the story. *Showing* is a great way to help your audience identify with a character's experience, especially if it's an experience your audience hasn't had. I don't know what it's like to feel miserable from tetanus, but I can easily imagine feeling so much pain that the least bit of light causes me to wince.

Pro Tips for "Showing" in a Forest Story

Forest Stories are easy traps for telling rather than showing. The very act of zooming out to the bigger context with information and data lends itself to more abstract language. One way to show rather than tell in a Forest Story is through strategic presentation of data.

While there are entire books dedicated to effective data visualization that you should read[33], one principle to keep in mind is that **the news is in the difference**. In other words, data *show* something when there is a point of comparison that causes something to stand out as different.

For example, the numbers this month are worse than last month; the numbers are notably different for one demographic than they are for another; the numbers indicate that one issue is more of a problem than another.

Notice how the data in the barge company story shows the problems because it offers comparisons. In the past, the American Barge Shipping Company achieved a 100 percent compliance score *compared to* its competitors, who scored no higher than 85 percent. In the past, American Barge ranked first in the industry compared to the present, when it ranks 13th.

So, presenting comparative data is a clever way to *show* rather than *tell* in a Forest Story.

In advocating for your cause, you want your audience to see and feel the problem you're asking them to act on. While telling them the problem is important, "telling" only activates the language centers of the brain. "Showing," however, engages more regions of the brain.

Metaphors and Analogies

A final strategy that is especially useful in getting Forest Stories to stick is the use of metaphors and analogies. These devices are really nothing more than the use of vivid, concrete imagery, but they're comparative rather than literal and are clever tools for making the generalized setting, characters, obstacles, and data of a Forest Story vivid.

In her 2021 TED Talk, "Tiny Balls of Fat That Could Revolutionize Medicine," Dr. Kathryn Whitehead was faced with the challenge of explaining to non-scientists how mRNA and *lipid nanoparticles* made the COVID-19 vaccines possible. The concepts and processes were highly abstract and virtually impossible for a lay audience to understand in a 20-minute TED Talk.[34]

Through a clever analogy, Whitehead explained the problem scientists faced in getting mRNA (the key ingredient of the vaccine) into cells, not just into muscles or the bloodstream. She compared mRNA to a fragile glass vase we'd like to send to someone through the mail, "without a box and bubble wrap." Like the unprotected glass vase, the mRNA would break before being delivered.

Building on the analogy, she added that it's also as if the mRNA has no address on the box and without an address, "your postal delivery service will have no idea where to take it." Knowing her audience would understand the vase conundrum, she was able to explain how her engineering team developed a delivery system for the mRNA that would allow it to arrive intact at the right location in the human body.

Where Whitehead's audience might not identify with the abstract biological concept of mRNA, they *could* identify with the image and experience of shipping a glass vase. The analogy served as a mini-story that made the concepts emotionally identifiable and memorable.

Metaphors and analogies can be powerful tools to help your audience remember and connect to important data points that support the mission you're advancing. If all else fails in making your Forest Story vivid, identifiable, concrete, and suspenseful, use a metaphor.

YOUR PATH FORWARD

When using stories to amplify and advocate for the change you want, you cannot afford to ignore techniques that impact the brain in ways that connect with human decision-making. Part of that challenge is making your stories enduring in the minds of your audience.

Once you decide the content in your Story Loop, go back and use at least three of these strategies to give your story Adhesives:

- **Make the characters vivid and identifiable.**
- **Build enough suspense** to create a need in your audience to know what happens next.
- **Add a few concrete sensory images** to help them see, hear, feel, smell, or taste important elements in the story.
- **Spot instances of telling** what a character feels, and find a way to show those feelings instead.
- **Find a metaphor or analogy** to help your audience see vividly anything abstract in your story.

Making even the smallest of adjustments through these techniques will pay dividends because the Adhesives make your stories memorable.

Chapter 8

BINDING

Tools to Connect the Parts of Your Stories

*A book falls apart without a strong binding. Likewise, a story
falls apart without a strong binding that holds the parts together.*

My young adult son and I have a common love of performing.
He performs as a slide guitarist in an up-and-coming band that
is touring the US, while I perform as a storyteller. So, it's not
uncommon for us to sit on our screened-in porch, talking into
the night about the challenges and joys of keeping an audience
in the palms of our hands for an hour or two at a time.

While our art forms differ, we share a conviction that having
the audience in the palm of one's hand isn't, or at least shouldn't
be, about one's ego. Rather, it's about the audience's experience.
When we achieve this goal, we know we've successfully pulled
them out of their day-to-day worlds, allowing them to temporarily leave behind their schedules, their to-do lists, their worries,

or the problems they need to solve. Instead, they're enraptured by the music or the characters in a story.

I'm often struck by the similarities in the behind-the-curtain techniques used by musical performers and storytellers. My son and his fellow band members have learned to strategically construct what they refer to as "the narrative of the show," which starts with how the band members walk onto the stage. They've learned the delicate and critical art of transitioning from one song to the next. And they've learned the importance of having just the right song to close the show and, when demanded by the crowd, what music to play for an encore.

So too, if you want your story to inspire your audience to act, you need them to be in the palm of your hand. To achieve this, you must strategically stitch together the parts of your story — the Normal, Uh-Oh, Intervention, and New Normal — with the right beginning, the right transitions, and the right ending. Three Binding techniques make all the difference in keeping your audience's attention: the Hook, Narrative Transitions, and the Exit.

THE HOOK: MAKE YOUR AUDIENCE CURIOUS

Several years ago, I was in the process of developing a Forest Story called "Digging in Their Heels" — a story performance of how women of the United States won the right to vote. Crafting this fact-filled story in a way that would keep audiences in the palm of my hand for an hour and inspire them to protect voting rights was a monumental challenge.

Once I had drafted the story, I sought the wise counsel of my storytelling coach, nationally acclaimed storyteller Beth Horner. Seared in my brain from our coaching session is the first piece of advice she offered. "Sally, you need to put your audience in a specific time and place right out of the gate."

What Beth had noted was the fact that the first few minutes of my story contained generalized statements about Americans not knowing much about how women won the vote. Unfortunately, this abstraction didn't captivate because it didn't put the audience into story mode. It sounded more like a lecture.

Upon hearing Beth's wisdom, I realized I'd forgotten what I knew from neuroscience: When stories put the audience in a vivid time and place and create some sense of "what's going to happen next?" the sensory and motor cortices are activated, cortisol is released, and they immediately pay attention.

In fact, research has shown that what happens in the first few seconds of a story impacts the audience's attention and receptivity to what is about to unfold. John Medina[35] and Vanessa Van Edwards[36] both found that capturing the audience's attention in the first few seconds with vivid statements that connect with their personal experience triggers the release of dopamine. This hormone, as you will recall, is key to audience engagement and decision-making. Additionally, the sooner the audience become curious about what's coming next, the better.

In sum, the hook of your story needs to *make your audience curious*, putting them in a setting of time and place as quickly as they start to wonder, "What's going to happen?"

> The hook of your story needs to *make your audience curious*, putting them in a setting of time and place as quickly as possible so they start to wonder, "What's going to happen?"

The Tree Tale Hook

When telling a Tree Tale, consider these two ways of hooking your audience.

Create Compelling Images of the Setting and Characters

In Chapter 5, you read the Tree Tale of Misha, Levi, and their daughter Savannah, who were impacted by the Ronald McDonald House. The story began with three sentences designed to hook the audience:

Sentence One: *Misha and Levi were small-town island musicians who lived on the Outer Banks of North Carolina.* — Immediately, the audience can envision the tourist island location.

Sentence Two: *As musicians, they lived a simple, low-income but joy-filled life entertaining tourists.* — Quickly, the audience can see the couple as musicians, living humbly and happily by making music.

Sentence Three: *When Misha and Levi married, they knew they would never have children because Misha once had breast cancer, and the treatments left her unable to conceive.* — By the third sentence, the audience is wondering where this is going (here comes the dopamine!) as they know there must be a reason that they're being told that the couple cannot conceive.

The Hook in this Tree Tale activates the sensory and motor cortices of the brain through a few vivid details that introduce the audience to a location and characters.

**Start with a Punchy Statement About the New Normal...
then Back Up.**

You can pique your audience's curiosity with a bold, perhaps unexpected statement about the New Normal that grabs their attention but then quickly backs up into the setting and characters. For example, in advocating for volunteer support at the Ronald McDonald house through this story, the hook might be a statement like this:

> **New Normal:** "I always knew the Ronald McDonald House provides families with good home-cooked meals, but I had no idea it also feeds their *souls*." **Back up to Normal:** "I had no idea, that is, until I learned about Misha and Levi. Misha and Levi were small-town island musicians who lived on the Outer Banks of North Carolina..."

Notice how this statement hooks the audience with a bold statement about the New Normal. The speaker's realization of the impact of the Ronald McDonald House piques curiosity, as the audience wonders, "What do you mean, it feeds their souls?" Such a statement needs to be short and striking to make the audience eager to know where the message is headed.

The Forest Story Hook: Three Techniques

It may be easy to see how to hook an audience in a close-up, personal Tree Tale, but what sort of hook can you use when working within a Forest Story's zoomed-out perspective? Here are three techniques.

Tell a Tree Tale

Unless you know your audience needs some data right away to perceive you as credible, you might start your Forest Story with a short Tree Tale as a hook.

For example, when determining what barriers were preventing patients from obtaining a newly launched medication from Innovate Pharma, the storytelling team analyzed AI-generated quantitative and qualitative data from the recorded patient-caregiver and service rep phone conversations, then crafted a story about the pain points.

Instead of starting the story with the Normal, which would clarify the date range and source of the data (the setting) as well as the types of people having the conversations with the agents (characters), the researchers started with a Tree Tale. They played the recorded parts of a conversation between a caregiver desperate to get her husband on the medication and a customer service representative. Instantly, the audience was hooked.

In fact, several found themselves in tears, saying things such as, "I've been working on this product launch but have never heard directly what it means to people."

After the hook, the storytellers backed into the Forest Story, starting with the Normal, explaining the data they analyzed, then shifting to the Uh-Oh, showing the prevalence of patients struggling through the financial process to afford the medication and struggling to find an infusion site that would administer the medication. Because of the hook, the audience eagerly followed along with the bigger story and were inspired to take action.

Make a Bold Statement

In the same way that you might start with a bold statement to make the audience curious before backing into a Tree Tale, you can also use a bold, unexpected statement to make the audience curious about a Forest Story.

Our Forest Story of the American Barge Company began like this:

> "American Barge Shipping Company was founded 79 years ago in 1946. And for 78 of those years, we held the track record for having the fewest accidents and fewest regulatory violations in the industry."

The hook might be more compelling, however, if it were a more startling statement like this:

> "It's not an option. We MUST reclaim our track record — not out of pride, but out of love.
>
> "American Barge was founded 79 years ago in 1946. And for nearly 80 years, we held the track record for having the fewest accidents and the fewest regulatory violations in the industry. That's an eight-decade record. Where our competitors achieved an 83 percent compliance score *at best*, we achieved a 100 percent compliance score year after year after year. Where our competitors experienced, on average, 3 deaths and 42 injuries annually, we experienced, on average, 0 deaths and 6 injuries annually."

The bold statement comes out of nowhere but makes the audience curious. What track record? Why is my CEO talking about love? Notice that the statement omits the word "safety" from the phrase "track record" to entice the audience to want to know more. Then the CEO quickly backs into the Forest Story, providing the data to show the Normal execution of safety protocols for nearly eight decades.

Pique Curiosity with a Metaphor

Another way to activate the release of dopamine early in a Forest Story is to use a vivid metaphor that can activate the brain's sensory and motor cortices in a way that data can't.

A metaphor hook might look like this:

> "Eight decades. That's the amount of time it takes to grow a redwood tree from a seed to 250 feet tall. Think about it. That's a long time.
>
> "In fact, that's how long we at American Barge Shipping Company held the industry record for employee safety. This company was founded nearly 80 years ago in 1946. And for 78 of those years, we held the track record for having the fewest accidents and the fewest regulatory violations in the industry. That's an eight-decade record."

The first three sentences stimulate curiosity as the audience is thinking, "Why is our CEO talking about redwood trees?" Then, as with the bold statement, the CEO backs into the Normal, explaining the company's success for so many years.

Whether using a Tree Tale, a bold statement about the New Normal, or a metaphor, the goal is the same: Make the audience need to know, "What's coming next?" Their dopamine will be flowing, and you'll have them in the palm of your hand.

Pro Tip on Story Hooks

Nothing diminishes the curiosity more than the statement, "Today, I want to tell you a story."

While you may need to give certain professional audiences a preview of what your data-specific Forest Story will cover, you still need a hook, whether at the beginning of your presentation or at the point when you launch into the details of the story.

When telling a Tree Tale, you're much more likely to captivate the audience by launching right into the curiosity statement or the specific setting rather than stating pleasantries like your thanks, your name, your credentials, or the weather.

NARRATIVE TRANSITIONS

Once you have your audience in the palm of your hand, you must keep them there. Language can make a major difference in whether or not you lose them. In both Tree Tales and Forest Stories, be sure to connect each part of the story with language that holds the narrative together.

For instance, imagine if a fairy tale sounded like this:

> "Once upon a time in a land far away, there was a king, queen, and princess. **And** every day, they went to the pond and ate their lunch. **And** as they walked around the pond, a frog jumped out and bit the princess's nose. **And** her nose kept growing. **And** then, a fairy godfather came and

told her to jump up and down three times. **And** her nose shrank to its normal size."

Did you read that and feel like you couldn't wait to know what happened next? Likely not. The parts of the story, as you can see, are linked with the word "and" again and again, which takes the Loop out of the story and turns it into a bulleted list.

Now, notice what happens when we change the language:

"Once upon a time in a land far away, there was a king, a queen, and a princess. Every day, they went to the pond and ate their lunch. **But then one day,** as they walked around the pond, a frog jumped out and bit the princess's nose. **Worse yet,** her nose kept growing, bigger and bigger and bigger. **Until finally,** along came a fairy godfather who told her to jump up and down three times. **Much to everyone's delight,** her nose shrank back to a normal size."

Notice the shift in language from "and" as the connector to the words "but then," "worse yet," "until finally," which convey a story. In his book *Storyworthy*, Matthew Dicks recommends this use of "but" and "therefore" language rather than "and" language to drive the audience to feel the suspense.[37] The "but" and "therefore" connectors help release the flow of dopamine, keeping your audience in the palm of your hand.

Narrative Transitions in Tree Tales

Let's return to our Ronald McDonald House story about Misha, Levi, and Savannah. Even if we leave out the details, when the narrative transitions are in place, we can see and feel the progression of the Story Loop.

- When Misha and Levi married, they knew they would never have children...
- **But one day,** they encountered a woman on the island who was pregnant... they brought Savannah home after her birth.
- **But within a few hours,** Savannah...
- **So,** they were grateful **when** they learned about the local Ronald McDonald House...
- **In fact, one night** at dinner... **At one point,** Misha looked over and saw...
- **Sadly,** Savannah lived only a few months longer, **but** Misha and Levi remain forever grateful...

The language of "but," "so," "then," and "at one point" turns what could have been a series of events strung together with the word "and" into a compelling narrative where the audience needs to know what happens next. When the audience is captivated throughout, you have a better chance of getting them to the end of the story, where they learn what they can do to support your mission.

Narrative Transitions in Forest Stories

You might naturally be inclined to use narrative transitions when telling a Tree Tale, especially if you were exposed to fairy tales as a young child. Most people, however, are less inclined to make natural use of narrative transitions when telling Forest Stories. For this, I blame the invention of PowerPoint back in 1987. When sharing data in a Forest Story, we often use slide decks and their built-in templates, which encourage the use of slide headers.

Slide headers serve an important function of orienting the audience to what they're seeing on the screen, but they tend to bury the narrative. They're like using the word "and" to string together the elements of a story. You've no doubt heard speakers say, "Now let's go to the next slide...," and "On this next slide you'll see...." But with this type of presentation, we're just trudging from slide to slide, with no narrative thread or suspense. When the storyline is unclear, the audience is no longer in the palm of the storyteller's hand, if they ever were.

So, just like Tree Tales, Forest Stories need narrative transitions in the form of "but," "since," "then," "so," and "therefore."

I once coached a woman, Ruth, who was giving a presentation on some research that she and a team had conducted to enhance the productivity of small coffee farms in Rwanda. She wanted to influence her audience to support other coffee farmers in developing countries. She had a sense that she needed to tell a story, but knew she was just stringing together a lot of data in a manner that wasn't inspiring.

After learning the Story Loop, Ruth stepped back from her data and figured out the narrative, re-designing her presentation as a story. She then courageously stepped out of her PowerPoint comfort zone. Instead of using only slides with headers for titles, she created narrative transition slides.

The first transition slide looked like this:

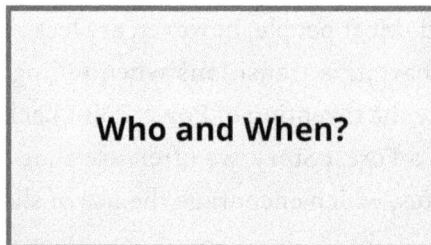

Who and When?

It was a clever way of saying "Once upon a time in a land far away" — in her case, referring to coffee farms in Rwanda.

After establishing the Normal, her second slide said this:

> ## A Gradual Decline

Uh-Oh! Something's awry in the production of coffee in Rwanda. She went on to present data to describe the problem, using a few additional transition slides to indicate the worsening of the problem. Then she transitioned with this:

> ## How Could We Help?

Here comes the Intervention, which she described using relevant data from their research.

Her final transition slide looked like this:

> ## So What Happened?

FROM STORY TO ACTION

The question led her audience right into the New Normal of the story.

Ruth was astounded, as were her colleagues, at how the very same data suddenly became compelling when the narrative transitions were featured rather than buried. These transitions deftly moved the audience through the Story Loop and kept them in the headspace of a story — gripped, not bored. The audience, now in the palm of her hand throughout her presentation, were much more likely to support her team's effort.

So, while the words "narrative transitions" may sound mundane, you can't afford to overlook them as you tell your stories. They're the glue that holds the parts of the Story Loop together.

> While the words "narrative transitions" may sound mundane, you can't afford to overlook them as you tell your stories. They're the glue that holds the parts of the Story Loop together.

THE EXIT

Once you've taken your audience from the Intervention into the New Normal, you need a way out of the story. Here are three strategies.

Cast Your Vision

If you're telling an Unfinished Story, especially if it's an Unfinished Forest Story, you must cast the vision of what the future could look like if action were taken. That vision needs to be clear, specific, and brief. Here's an example:

> "If we can build this community center, we are confident we'll see three results: 1) At least a 40 percent reduction in neighborhood crime; 2) Job opportunities for more than 100 community members; and 3) Healthier families and a tighter-knit community. Why would we ever say no to that?"

Notice that the vision is specific: three simple but clear outcomes hoped for in the construction of a community center. Notice, too, that there's a simple, strong statement at the end, which signals that the story is over and reinforces the value of the vision.

Make Your Ask

The exit may be the time in your story to ask your audience for the specific support you need. Here, your audience becomes a character in your story, and your task is to make them feel like a valuable participant in advancing your noble cause. Notice this slight twist on the example above:

> "If we can build this community center, we are confident we'll see three results: 1) At least a 40 percent reduction in neighborhood crime; 2) Job opportunities for over 100 community members; and 3) Healthier families and a tighter-knit community. Why would we ever say no to that?

"So today, we ask you to consider saying 'yes' to lower crime, to job opportunities, and to healthy families in our neighborhood by giving a one-time gift of whatever size you're able, knowing that your gift will turn our community into the place we all want to call home."

In this example, the vision is cast with precision and brevity. A statement of inspiration is offered to get the audience to think about their response to the vision. Then, a simple call to action is made and linked directly to the vision. Finally, the story ends with a statement of motivation: "Your gift will turn our community into the place we all want to call home." No ambiguity, no beating around the bush with the request, no wandering around to get to the request.

Keep It Brief

In the same way that there's no better way to stomp out your audience's curiosity than by beginning with the phrase, "I'd like to tell you a story," there's no better way to ruin your story than by going on too long.

Let the story do its work! If the story was truly compelling, the audience doesn't need you to interpret it for them or for you to re-explain the value of your mission. The story told them.

If you carry on with a long ending, you shift from storytelling to preaching. While there's certainly a

> Let the story do its work! If the story was truly compelling, the audience doesn't need you to interpret it for them.

time and place for preaching, it's not when you're asking your audience to support your objective.

Moreover, once you're to the point of casting the vision or making an ask, the suspense of your story is over, the dopamine and cortisol are slowing down, and the audience's attention will quickly wane. You can't afford to risk losing them from the palm of your hand.

So, let the Story Loop do its job. If you're telling an Unfinished Story, cast your vision. If you need to make an ask, put out the call to action. Know your final statement. And most importantly, keep it brief.

YOUR PATH FORWARD

You can craft a story with all the components of the Story Loop and make it sticky with all the Adhesive techniques. But if you ignore the Binding tools, your audience will inevitably drift off to their grocery list instead of listening, skip paragraphs instead of reading, and scroll on to the next image on social media instead of watching.

Yet binding doesn't come naturally to most of us.

Once you have shaped the content of your narrative plan, practice these three strategies:

- **Create a vivid Hook** that will entice them immediately.
- **Formulate Narrative Transitions** that deliberately and logically link each component of your story.
- **Devise a compelling Exit** that clarifies the vision/ask and leaves the audience inspired.

What you're advocating for matters. Keeping your audience in the palm of your hand is not about boosting your ego — it is about achieving your noble cause. You can't afford to let them escape.

Chapter 9

ALIGNMENT

Adapting Your Stories to Align with Your Audience

Driving a car with the wheels out of alignment makes it difficult to go in the right direction. So does telling stories that are out of alignment with your audience.

In my storytelling workshops, clients excitedly get to work using the Story Loop to craft their Tree Tales or Forest Stories. Then, inevitably, at some point, their practical brains take over and they begin asking questions like:

- What's the best mechanism for delivering our stories? Should they be written? Should they be told verbally? Should they be told in a video?
- How long should our stories be?
- Is one platform better than another for Tree Tales vs. Forest Stories?

My answers always remind me of driving a vehicle in a Midwestern urban area in the months of February and March. It's like being that metal ball in a pinball machine, ricocheting back and forth. For at least eight weeks, you keep your eyes on the road, gripping both hands on the wheel as you swerve side to side on the road, dodging the dreaded potholes.

The greatest pothole danger occurs when driving at night or early in the morning before sunrise. Some of those nasty craters are impossible to see in the dark, especially if they're filled with rainwater. So, it's no surprise that one March morning, I was driving to an early coffee meeting when I hit one... hard.

But as one does, I kept driving, hoping there was no damage. After only an hour at the coffee shop, I walked out to my car, having forgotten all about the pothole. Without thinking to check the tires, I hopped in the car and headed down the road. But within seconds, I knew something was terribly wrong.

The steering wheel was fighting me just to drive straight down a flat city street. I could tell the tire had very little air, and I could barely keep the car moving in a forward direction. As you've probably guessed, my wheels were now out of alignment due to the pothole.

Later that day, I was thinking about the similarity between tire alignment and audience alignment with storytelling. When I'm asked these tactical questions about storytelling in my workshops, my immediate goal is to redirect the thinking from "formula" (for delivery mechanism, length, platform) to "principle" — the principle of Alignment.

Just as your car tires need to be aligned to get you to your destination, if you want to successfully advocate and influence, your stories need to be aligned with your target audiences. When you think strategically about who your target audience is and what you want from them, the answers to practical questions about your delivery mechanism, length, and platform become clear.

So, let's get practical about what you need to consider regarding your audience.

FIVE QUESTIONS TO ASK ABOUT YOUR AUDIENCE

To determine your story type, length, delivery mechanism, and platform, you can use the journalist's five questions: who, what, where, when, and why.

But unlike a journalist, you're in the business of persuasion. So, the "why" question must be your first rather than your last.

Why Do You Want Them to Hear Your Story?

Get clarity on exactly what you want from your audience. The more clearly you define your desired outcome, the more clearly you know how the story must be delivered.

As you define your desired outcome, identify both the implicit and explicit layers of what you want from your audience. For example, at one level, you might say, "I want my audience to support my cause" by, for example, following a new rule, donating money, passing legislation, changing a procedure, or volunteering. This layer of the ask dictates exactly who needs to hear the story and whether they need to be together in one space with you or they can receive this story outside your presence.

But you might also want something underneath this ask. Perhaps you also want your audience to engage in your Unfinished Story by discussing, debating, and deciding on the course of action you propose. Perhaps you're reaching an audience who then needs to influence others who will ultimately make the decision. The need for their participation, or not, would dictate a different platform for telling the story.

Take, for example, the American Barge story from Chapter 5. The hypothetical company Forest Story is told by the CEO *not* to generate discussion or debate but to motivate employees to comply. A video would work well for such a story, as it could be shared multiple times and is intentionally a unidirectional form of communication.

But if you're proposing the new safety regulations to members of the American Barge C-Suite, and you *want* debate and discussion, a live telling of the story is most strategic. With that approach, the target audience can talk about the proposal, ask questions, and come to a decision.

Rule of Thumb: The bigger your ask, the more direct and personal the delivery of your story needs to be.

If you're asking your audience for something that costs them little — give $10, volunteer two hours, attend a few meetings — your channel can be less personal: social media, a newsletter, a blog. Because the audience's investment is small, they don't require as much data as evidence of your impact, and you won't have to tailor your story to their specific needs or interests.

But if you are asking a select group of donors for large sums of money or senior leaders for a budget expansion or your team leaders for a process change, they potentially have a lot to lose by supporting your cause. In such cases, your personal connection is critical in lending credibility to the cause.

In essence, the bigger the ask, the more you and the story need to connect with your audience's interests and concerns, and that connection will have maximum impact if your story is told live and in person.

Who Are They and Why Would They Be Interested?

The more you know about those with whom you are communicating, the more you can tailor your story and its delivery to have maximum impact. Specifically, consider the following:

Psychographics

First and foremost, pay attention to your audience's psychographics — their beliefs, values, interests, motivations, and personality traits. What do those pre-existing psychographics tell you about how you should adapt both the content and the delivery of your story? This does not mean you should avoid challenging their beliefs or values. Nor does it mean you should relinquish the truth of your story to cater to them. In fact, psychographics helps you do just the opposite. You won't know how to challenge assumptions if you don't know what they might be.

Let's say, for example, you're seeking support from City Council members to build a post-incarceration rehabilitation center in a particular neighborhood. The more you know about the council members' motivations and interests, the more you can shape your Story Loop so the New Normal appeals not only to the interests of those you represent, but also to the interests and motivations of your audience — e.g., those in the audience concerned with neighborhood safety, those interested in business development, or those focused on neighborhood aesthetics.

Knowing the council members' interests and motivations might also influence whether you need to tell a Tree Tale with identifiable characters that build sympathy or whether you need a Forest Story that offers broader context. It might also dictate how you creatively design your story so that you connect with the audience's interests and motivations early in the narrative, so as not to lose their interest or get them mentally arguing with you before you get to your New Normal.

Knowing whether your audience is already interested or whether you must persuade them to be interested in your mission will guide you in shaping your story to connect with their interests and values. It will also guide you in deciding whether they're likely to invest much time in reading, watching, or listening to your story.

Position or Role

Consider the role held by those to whom you are telling your story. Are you telling a story to persuade senior leadership in your company, and are you below them in the hierarchy? Or are you telling a story to your peers or the team that reports to you in the hierarchy? Are you telling the story to legislators who hear hundreds of pleas for legislative support, or are you telling the story to convince fellow believers in your cause to volunteer at an event?

Each of these scenarios will dictate different story lengths and delivery systems. Senior leaders and legislators will likely have limited time and patience for a long story, whereas others may crave a longer story with more context that gives them the details and context they need.

Your Relationship to Your Audience

Ask yourself whether your audience knows you and your organization or team, or if you are unknown. If you are known, consider the nature of your relationship and how well they know you.

The more direct your relationship, the more personal your delivery mechanism must be. Recall from Chapter 2 that storytelling can result in "neuro-coupling" — a syncing of the brain activity between storyteller and story receiver. That coupling is more likely to occur when the receiver sees and hears the face and voice of the storyteller.

Demographics

Identify relevant demographic variables in your audience: Age, gender, race/ethnicity, income level, education level, geographic location, occupation, religion, and so forth. Then, look at your story to see where there might be disparities between the way the story is told and any of those demographics.

For example, a university seeking to recruit students may need to adapt its impact stories differently for high school juniors of a particular race in a particular geographic region scrolling on social media than for the parents attending a college prep night at their child's high school. So too, a prospective university donor in their 40s who is of a particular gender, ethnicity, and occupation is different than a prospective donor who is in their 80s and of a different ethnicity and occupation. Your story must consider what content would or would not be understood by or important to these different groups.

Considering these demographics might also help you decide which delivery methods or platforms would be most desirable for this audience to access. What would be the easiest way for them to consume your story?

Demographic adaptation does not mean that the truth of the story should differ from audience to audience, but it may mean that the length, the vocabulary, and the references within the story should be adapted.

What Do They (Not) Know About Your Cause?

Oh, how easy it is to assume the audience knows more than they do about your purpose. You assume they know about the problem your mission addresses. You assume they know about the types of individuals and needs of those you serve. You assume they know who you are. You assume they're familiar with the history or inner workings of your organization.

Not only might *you* assume your audience knows more than they do, but it's also likely that *your audience* assume they know more than they actually do about your cause. They think they know whom you serve, how you accomplish your mission, your resources, your impact. But gaps in their knowledge may be impacting the decisions they are or are not willing to make to support your goals.

As you reflect on your story, aim to see it through the eyes of someone who may not know your context and mission as you do.

Say, for example, that you represent a state government agency like the Department of Transportation. You need to go before the State Senate to advocate for an increase in your next year's budget, so you put together a great Forest Story that shows the Normal from the past three years and the Uh-Oh of how the limited budget has impeded the department's ability to service the licensing needs of truck drivers. This impairment has negatively impacted businesses.

The story makes perfect sense to you, but your audience includes newly elected legislators who come from varied backgrounds, so they're not well educated on the licensing functions of the Department of Transportation. For the narrative to make as much sense to your audience as it does to you, you must ensure the context, definitions, and explanations they need are present.

Or let's say you represent a nonprofit theatre organization that offers six community programs ranging from mainstage productions to youth summer theatre camps to military veterans' acting classes. The potential donors attending your annual fundraising think they know your theatre's mission because they regularly attend mainstage performances. Unbeknownst to them, however, are the other five programs, which have the biggest community impact.

Knowing your audience's lack of a deeper awareness, you might use a variety of platforms to tell multiple stories throughout your event, thus having more impact.

When you consider the information your audience *lacks* about your mission, you can invent creative ways to tell your story, perhaps in more than one setting via more than one platform. This approach will educate your audience over time, thus preparing them for the key story to have more impact.

Do all you can to avoid assumptions.

Where Can Your Audience Most Effectively Engage with Your Story?

What you want your story to prompt the audience to do — including sharing your story — helps determine the optimal location for them to encounter it.

For example, if you want them to make a small $25 donation, choose a platform that will quickly convey the story and enable the receiver to take action with ease. If you want them to approve the budget increase you're proposing for the upcoming fiscal year, you may want them together in a physical space to discuss it, where they can also see the necessary supporting documents.

Furthermore, knowing where you want them to be when they encounter your story can guide your decisions about length, platform, and delivery mechanism.

- Will they be in a space where they will be easily distracted?
- Will they be a captive audience in a space where their attention will inherently be focused?
- Will they be in a meeting online where they're tempted to multitask?

- Will they be alone or with others?
- Will they be in a place where they're quickly scrolling through emails or social media?
- Will they be in a space where they're focused, quiet, and able to give full attention to a story?

The physical context in which your audience will encounter your story can guide you on an appropriate story length. Will they be in a location that allows for in-depth reading? Will they be in a space that accommodates only quick, cursory scrolling through messages? Will they be in a space that allows for social interaction around and about your story?

Wherever you anticipate your audience is, consider this fact about people: For most of human history, we've been oral storytellers. In fact, we've only been writing our stories for a few thousand years (relatively little in the span of all time), and we weren't *readers* of stories until the invention of the printing press in 1440. Even at that, widespread literacy across most social classes has only been around for about 600 years.

Moreover, technology of the past 20 years has caused yet another shift: We've reverted to oral storytelling thanks to video technologies. While our storytelling isn't live around a campfire, it's often conveyed orally via video. We are wired for oral storytelling.

That said, the psychographics and demographics of your audience will dictate whether your story should be delivered in writing, orally in person, or orally via video. Some audiences prefer to read. Others prefer to watch. And the location in which an audience is situated will dictate whether written or oral messages are accessible or convenient.

If your story *is* best conveyed in writing, use plenty of visual support with photos, easy-to-interpret graphs, and subheads that contain the narrative transitions, so your audience feels as much like they're in a story as they would if they were hearing it live.

When and How Often Do They Need to Hear Your Story?

Consider whether your audience needs to encounter this story just once or multiple times. This factor may be influenced by whether your ask is urgent or requires deliberation.

For example, when advocating for their company to change its communication process to target the consumer rather than the physicians, the Innovate Pharma storytelling team knew the change would require support from senior leadership, legal counsel, marketing, and field representatives. The team built a convincing data-backed Forest Story that successfully convinced leaders from across the company to invest over a million dollars in a website redesign and campaign to reach patients directly.

But the convincing didn't happen overnight.

For three months, the team told the story over and over again, modifying it for different internal audiences and repeating it to others, tweaking and altering it to become more convincing, until finally the decision scales were tipped.

If the decision you want your audience to make requires similar collective or individual deliberation, they may need to encounter the story more than once. If so, you will need multiple versions of it to avoid redundancy. You may, for example, want a written version for an annual publication or magazine, and you may also want a video version to share on social media.

If you need to tell the story more than once, ask yourself when the audience will be most receptive to it or when you most need them to hear it again. Space the time between story encounters so that the audience will be drawn in for a second, third, or fourth time.

Remember, even if you feel you've saturated your audience with too many story encounters, in truth, the number is probably not nearly enough. In most instances, the more often an audience hears the same compelling story, the more likely they are to take action.

MULTIPLE VERSIONS GIVE YOU FLEXIBILITY

I once heard a master storyteller say, "It takes at least four minutes to tell a great story." I've thought about and often questioned that advice as I've worked with hundreds of clients on their storytelling for all sorts of worthy purposes. I've reached a Goldilocks conclusion:

The story length needs to be *just right.*

The best way to set yourself up for *just right* is to have a long version and a short version (maybe even a medium version) of the story that you can adapt for different audiences in different contexts at different points in time.

For example, in my workshops, participants begin crafting Tree Tales and Forest Stories about their noble cause, using the Story Loop structure. Each storyteller is encouraged to develop the story in full, with as much detail as possible.

Once they've sketched a version of their story, they tell the full, detailed story to others in the group who behave as the target audience. In that role, the listeners give feedback from the perspective of the target audience, pointing out how the story might better speak to their interests or pointing out what assumptions the storyteller made about the audience's knowledge.

After each storyteller receives several rounds of feedback, they're asked to engage in a "speed storytelling" exercise akin to "speed dating," in which everyone must tell their story in two minutes or less. The speed storytelling activity forces each storyteller to know the bones of the story and discover which elements they must include and which they can afford to leave out.

While you can get through the Story Loop in 30 seconds in an elevator pitch, a social media post, or a commercial, if you want to compel your audience to act on your cause, you may need more detail to activate their brains' decision-making centers. This doesn't necessarily require a 20-minute story, but it does mean your story needs to be long enough to include details that address mental objections or questions that might otherwise prevent them from taking the desired action.

If you create a long and short version of your story and get feedback from your team members, you will learn what cannot be dropped if the story is to still have impact, and what details are compelling but not necessary if time or space is limited.

Having multiple versions of the story prepares you to easily adapt the story for different platforms, delivery mechanisms, and purposes.

What's Worth Lengthening and Shortening

When deciding what to excise or expand in your story, remember the principles behind the Story Loop structure. The heart of the story lies in the Uh-Oh, getting the audience to feel the characters' pain, and the Intervention, helping the audience see how the pain was eliminated, or could be.

Remember, too, that the suspense is in the Uh-Oh phase of the story. That's when your audience's cortisol starts to elevate and dopamine is released, causing them to forget all else and pay attention to the story as they anticipate the satisfaction that comes from a resolution.

Because the Uh-Oh captures attention and shows the problem, and because the Intervention proves your mission does or will solve the problem, those two components of the story need more development than the Normal and New Normal.

In fact, if the Normal lasts too long, the lack of suspense will make the audience quickly check out. So, establish what the audience needs — introduction of time, place, characters, and what's been the norm — quickly. Then get to the Uh-Oh.

Once they've reached the story's end, the New Normal must also be brief. Here's an example of why.

I once sat at a luncheon event where a speaker told a story about her experience with a charitable organization. After a good 30 minutes of speaking, she gave us an ending cue we were all quite ready for.

She said, "So the final chapter was..."

Ahhhhh, I thought. *She's about to wrap it up.*

But no.

She talked on for another five minutes, then said, "But the final, final chapter was..."

REALLY? She's not done? Oh well. Now she's at the end.

Then she said (I'm not making this up), "But the real final chapter was..."

NOOOOOOOO! NOOOOOOO!

There were FIVE "final chapters" to the story. I wanted to squirm out of my seat and crawl to the door.

To keep your audience from sliding out of their seats, know and respect the appropriate length of time to deliver your story orally or in writing, and plot the length of each component of the Story Loop strategically.

If you have four minutes to tell your story, don't assume that each of the four components of the Loop should get a minute. Instead, give the Normal 30 seconds, the Uh-Oh and Intervention three minutes, and the New Normal 30 seconds. Use the same basic distribution if you're allowed 10 minutes, 30 minutes, or 500 written words.

Don't ignore the fact that your audience's brains function differently during the Normal and New Normal of your story. No matter how much time or space you're allotted, give them what they need but no more.

YOUR PATH FORWARD

Before, during, and after you craft your story, ask these questions:

- **Who is your audience?** What matters to them, and what is your relationship with them?
- **Why do you want them to hear this story?** To deliberate, discuss, decide, remember?
- **What do they (not) know about your mission?** What should you not assume?
- **Where will they be when they encounter your story?** In a space where they'll invest time and energy or in a space that requires speed?
- **When do you need them to encounter your story?** Now? Or now and later? If later, when?
- **Should you craft a long and a short version?** Will the story be repurposed?
- **Have you maintained the heart of the story?** Are the Uh-Oh and Intervention front and center, no matter what delivery system is used?

In the same way that your car will only get you to your destination efficiently if the wheels are aligned, your story will only get you to your desired outcome if it's aligned with your audience's needs and context.

Whenever you begin asking tactical questions about the mechanisms through which you will deliver your story, shift your mindset from formulas to the principle of Alignment with your audience. Only then can you avoid the potholes.

Chapter 10

PRESERVATION

Cataloguing and Tracking Your Stories

Not organizing your photos is regrettable.
Not organizing your stories is equally regrettable.

Nobody ever says, "Boy, I'm sure glad I never organized my photos. I love digging through that shoebox stuffed with old prints, trying to find some photo I think I remember. And I just love having those pictures haphazardly scattered across my devices. It's like a scavenger hunt every time I open my photo app! I'm so glad I never took time to organize all that."

Nope. Nobody ever says that.

Now, you may very well be one of those people who never allow their photos to get disorganized. Maybe you're like my admirable cousin who dedicates his weekends to organizing the photos in an online album in chronological order, labeling them by date and occasion, noting the ages of his kids at each event. Maybe you have a routine practice of going through your photos on your phone, deleting duplicates, organizing them by theme, and creating categories so you can find what you're looking for.

Or maybe you're like me. You're talking with a friend who wants to see a photo from that wedding several months back, and you start scrolling, scrolling, scrolling through your photos, saying, "Hang on, I know it's in here somewhere." Meanwhile, your friend has moved on to a completely different topic while you still have your nose buried in the mess of photos. Yup, that's me.

Are you running into the same kind of situation with your stories? If they've become like the shoebox, a random mess in which you can't find anything, let alone use it again, you probably need a cataloguing system that helps you more effectively repurpose them.

This comes in the form of what I call a Story Vault, which will not only help you curate and track your deployment of stories but will also help cultivate a storytelling culture around your noble cause.

THE VALUE OF A STORY VAULT

At Authenticx, as I mentioned in Chapter 2, I work with a team of data-backed storytellers who analyze data from millions of unstructured conversations, turning them into compelling stories that help healthcare companies improve their patient and customer experience. Each storyteller crafts and delivers on average six Forest Stories per month. The team often jokes that the minute they finish a storytelling session with a client, the story contents get shoved into a sub-atomic-sized crevice in the backs of their brains as they immediately turn to the next story project.

Fortunately, one clever member of the storytelling team thought to create a shared "Tome of Stories" — a simple Excel document in which each storyteller could keep track of the stories they present and easily reference them in the future. In the tome, we record several details about the stories: client, delivery date, title, story focus, links to the deck, and links to any recordings of the storytelling session.

The 15 minutes it takes to fill in the tome pays dividends for the entire team down the road. At some point, we inevitably find ourselves crafting a story that's akin to something we told in the past. The tome prevents us from recreating the wheel, as we can borrow metaphors, data visualizations, and story structures from existing documents. When another storyteller or someone from sales or marketing asks, "Have any of you told a story about X?" we can direct them to the tome for samples. When a new employee joins the team, we can direct them to the tome for models of how stories are structured. The resource is invaluable not only to each storyteller but to the company at large.

Not all advocacy work entails a collection of stories. You might, for example, from time to time need to advocate for a business change to your senior leadership. Or, on occasion, you may need to motivate your team with a story. In these cases, you develop and tell a story for that specific purpose, then move on.

On the other hand, your advocacy work may require ongoing storytelling. Perhaps you lead a school within a university. You and your team have a perpetual need to tell compelling stories for student and faculty recruitment, fundraising, and alumni relations. Or perhaps you are part of an organization in which your employees and board members must tell stories to the community to garner support for your mission.

If there's a chance that you and your team will tell many stories to advance your cause, you need to develop a robust story tome, vault, bank, or repository. We'll call the general version of it a Story Vault, but feel free to use whatever title rings best for you.

THE CONTENTS OF THE STORY VAULT

Your vault needs to contain not only the stories themselves (links to recorded or written versions of the story, slide decks, etc.) but also a cataloging system that tracks information about the contents and usage of each story. No matter which platform you choose (Microsoft Excel, Google Docs, cloud databases, digital asset managers, or hybrid work management systems), you need a basic spreadsheet-type listing that allows you to record what you and your team will want to reference about each story. While the contents will vary depending on your needs, here's a checklist of what many organizations find valuable in their tracking system.

Story Title

Giving each story a non-obscure title makes it easy to scan and find that story months after its creation. Here are some examples based on the sample stories you've read in this book:

- *EV Origin Story*
- *Impact of Employee Ownership on Custodian*
- *Child Makes a Friend at Ronald McDonald House*
- *Dare to Care Story*
- *Failure of HCP Communication Strategy*
- *Patient Portal Access Story*
- *Rwandan Coffee Impact Story*

While these titles represent different types of organizations, each contains something specific enough for an individual familiar with the story to understand and recall its gist. If someone seeking a story is unfamiliar, they can glean from the title whether the story is worth exploring.

Story Source and Consent Details

Keep track of whose story is being told, who created the story, and who delivered the story. This is especially important if the source of the story differs from its creator and deliverer.

When tracking a Tree Tale, you need a system for honoring the consent principals discussed in Chapter 5. Be sure to identify the following:

- Original source: Whose story is it?
- Who crafted the story?
- Who tells the story? (Third-person narrator? First-person?)
- Contact information of the source (so you can reach them should you want to use the story again for different purposes).
- Link to signed consent for use of the story.
- History of who has contacted the source and when (so you can refer to that contact should you need to ask permission for new uses of that individual's story).

When tracking a Forest Story, record the following so you have the necessary resources should the story need to be updated or repurposed:

- Who was responsible for gathering any data in the Forest Story?
- What were the data sources?
- Who crafted the story?
- Who delivered the story?

Date Gathered

A record of the date the story was crafted or gathered from the source enables your team to assess whether the story is potentially outdated or whether a refresh is needed with any data gathered. Interview dates and notes give clues as to whether the individuals should be contacted again to ensure the story is still up to date.

Story Scope

Tag the story as a Tree Tale, Forest Story, or a combination so your team can sort for the type of story and quickly eliminate those with an inappropriate scope for their purpose and context.

Story Type

Tag the story for one of the following Story Types explained in Chapter 3: Origin, Impact, Hurdle, Motivation, Cautionary, or Unfinished. Your team will thank you when they can sort to find a story that would fit their current purpose and eliminate stories that wouldn't work.

In addition to tagging with the generic Story Types, you should also keep notes on the specific utility of the story. For example, you might indicate Impact Story as the type, and also make note of the story's value for a particular goal. An Impact Story for a fundraising goal, for example, would be different than an Impact Story for a recruitment goal or a team motivational goal. Notes like this can help your team:

This story is great for the capital campaign because it features the impact of the current, limited laboratory space.

OR

This story is great for helping people understand the problems we solve at a high level. Not great for buyers who know the industry and want details, but great for employees who need to understand and value the business model.

OR

This story shows the impact of our work on kids, but not on parents or the schools themselves.

Notations like these about the utility of the story can save team members hours of sifting and sorting.

Story Usage

To prevent a redundant use or overuse of a story, make notes on *where* the story has been shared. If it was told at a fundraising event, track that. If it was shared via video in a newsletter and a blog post, note that. If it was posted on social media sites, record that.

If you're part of a large organization, be alert to the fact that different functional areas may use the same stories in different ways. You may want to create a system for checking across departments to ensure stories are being used appropriately and strategically throughout the organization, and for tracking their use by other departments.

Tracking the specific *dates* when stories were disseminated makes it easy to decide down the road whether sufficient time has elapsed for a story to be used again.

If necessary, clarify who the *audience* was for the story. For example, if the story was delivered live, be sure to specify the nature of the audience. Such records ensure that your storytelling stays fresh for audiences you communicate with regularly.

Platform/Channel

Track the platform or communication channel used for the delivery of the story. Simple categories might include:

- In-person presentation
- Video for event
- Video for Instagram, Facebook, LinkedIn
- Video for TikTok
- Article for newsletter
- Article for blog
- Article for magazine
- Recorded presentation

Story Length

Keep track of the story length. If written, notate the number of words. If oral, note the time length. Again, your team will thank you for this sorting mechanism to find what they need for a new purpose.

Story Summary

Brief summaries are invaluable for expediting another team member's search through the Story Vault. The team member responsible for the creation of the story should write a brief 1–3 sentence summary of the story content. A summary might be as simple as these:

> *Story of Misha and Levi's experience at the Ronald McDonald House, where their daughter signed the word "friend" to another child, showing how the RMH provides community as well as food and shelter to families managing illness of a child.*

OR

Story with data that show how patients are delayed in getting on our medication because physicians' competing priorities have been impeding their communication. Quantitative data prove prevalence of the problem; qualitative data provide evidence from patient voices of their frustration. Story proposes a new approach of direct patient contact.

Summaries like these are quickly searchable in digital asset management systems or cloud databases.

Relevant Links

Links to any recording or documentation of the story are a gift to another team member looking to use, modify, or learn from an existing story. Be sure to include links to video recordings of the story, written documents of the story, slide decks supporting the story, or online locations of the story.

I recommend creating a long and short version of the story that a user can access and modify for different audiences, purposes, and platforms. Linking to the short and long versions gives others quick access to the content needed.

ASSIGNING A STORY CURATOR

You may be reading about the Story Vault, envisioning how this could be useful for your team but also thinking to yourself, "A Story Vault is a great idea, but who's going to execute it? Is this the marketing team's responsibility? Should someone else be the story organizer?"

Yes, Someone Must be Appointed

The *first* answer to the question of ownership is quite simply: Yes, *someone* must be appointed to oversee the construction and maintenance of the Story Vault. Think of this person as the museum curator who keeps track of the inventory of artifacts. Who that person should be, however, depends on the size and structure of your team or organization and what you envision as your larger storytelling strategy.

Here are three curator responsibilities that can significantly help an organization coordinate its storytelling.

First, the curator should be an employee or member of the organization who is responsible for creating and maintaining the story database. While the curator may ask other members of the organization to add their story data into the document, the curator ensures the details are clear, sufficient, and accessible. In other cases, the curator may be assigned to do all the documentation for the database, which offloads the burden from those crafting and telling the stories.

Second, the curator should know which functional areas of an organization are using stories so they can schedule regular check-ins to be sure all relevant story information is being captured in the database.

Third, the curator should be responsible for checking all consent information in the database to ensure compliance with the organization's ethical standards for the use of individuals' stories.

The weight of a curator's responsibilities will vary depending on the size of your organization and the volume of stories you produce. But assigning this work to someone who will hold your team accountable will make the system sustainable, functional, and timesaving for everyone.

Decide How Your Organization Should Coordinate Storytelling

There's a second answer to the question of assigning a curator, which is another question: How do you want your organization to coordinate, collaborate, and strategize around storytelling?

If, in fact, you're now convinced that storytelling is a necessary tool for your advocacy, you need to consider how you want your story strategy to work for your team at large. The Story Vault is simply a tool for this larger strategy.

I have found that when teams are given the storytelling tools taught in this book, they typically discover that the work of storytelling ought not be compartmentalized in the marketing division alone. The more cross-functionally equipped team members are to tell both Forest Stories and Tree Tales, the more broadly the group's worthwhile purpose can be amplified.

When a wide range of people in your organization share a common storytelling vocabulary with phrases like "Story Loop," "Forest Stories," "Tree Tales," "Unfinished Stories," "Hurdle Stories," and "Adhesive," suddenly there is potential for a coordinated vision of the types of stories that need to be crafted and delivered for different purposes, audiences, and contexts. The more team members there are who can both speak the language and create stories using those tools, the more stories you will have available to drive action. When this happens, the marketing team functions not in isolation but in collaboration with other team members who are developing and using stories for both internal and external purposes.

When marketers and employees from other parts of the business or organization, as well as board members and volunteers, share a common vision for storytelling, the question of who should curate the Story Vault typically answers itself. You'll know which person or role in your organization is the most logical for overseeing and maintaining the records.

Value Add: Story Vaults Spark Storytelling Cultures

While an essential tool for organizing a growing collection of advocacy stories and ensuring their strategic use, a Story Vault can also serve as a catalyst for the development of a storytelling culture within your business or organization. This, in fact, may be its greater function.

Consider this analogy. The world's great religions all have sacred texts that are central to each faith. Those texts are, in many ways, a vault of stories that unite the faithful. Religious leaders draw from the vaults over and over again, pulling different stories for different purposes, rituals, and lessons. The collection of stories is central to the community, ensuring its continuity from generation to generation.

While the stories you tell to advocate for your purpose may not be as sacred or timeless as the ancient scriptures, the very act of collecting and curating your stories, using a common vocabulary for Story Types and scopes, can result in the same kind of cultural shift. The more you and your team become strategic storytellers, the greater your influence will be, both internally and externally.

For example, using the clients' data, the storytelling team at Authenticx creates and tells stories that give clients insights to improve their business outcomes. But after delivering the stories to the clients, the storytellers often share the stories back with the Authenticx employees, which has great benefits:

- The revenue team is equipped with Impact Stories to share with prospects.
- The marketing team is equipped with Impact Stories to share in digital marketing campaigns.
- The platform development team is inspired to build new features.
- Overall company motivation is reignited upon hearing the stories of impact.

In essence, a storytelling culture impacts the business all the way around.

As team members contribute to the Vault, they can see gaps in the types of stories needed, encouraging proactive efforts to find and create new stories, or they see the value of certain Story Types over others. The repository, in essence, can unify and empower your team with common resources and a shared vision for how stories can be used to amplify your cause.

YOUR PATH FORWARD

You may now be envisioning your Story Vault and possibly have a good person in mind to serve as Story Curator. You may even be inspired by the vision of a storytelling culture to help advance your mission.

Get started with these steps:

- **Create a spreadsheet (or other similar organization system in your platform of choice)** with the relevant categories and complete one row for the first story you have told.
- **Challenge your team to add a story** each time they tell or create one that advances your mission.
- **Make the Story Vault visible** so the team is inspired to see it grow.
- **Remember the awful alternative**: haphazardly stored stories, duplicate efforts, abuse of story sources, and inappropriate manipulation of stories.

Failing to build a thoughtful Story Vault will inevitably create problems you can avoid. Your effort will pay off.

Nobody ever said, "I'm so glad I never organized my photos." And nobody who's telling Tree Tales and Forest Stories to advocate for a critically important purpose will ever say, "I'm so glad I never organized those stories."

Keep your stories out of the shoebox!

Chapter 11

THE 10 ESSENTIAL
STORYTELLING RULES

*Now that you've read the playbook with lots of tips
and tricks... don't get too hung up on them.*

True confession that may sound weird coming from the author: I have a love-hate relationship with books like this — books chock full of useful frameworks, strategies, techniques, formulas, and tools for helping me develop professionally and personally.

Here's the love part: I love it when such a book speaks to a real gap in my mindset or skillset. I love it when such a book puts a new spin on something I've considered for a long time. I especially love it when such a book challenges me to think in entirely new ways, forcing me to reconsider my beliefs, values, habits, or behaviors. No doubt you, like me, can name the top three to five books that have had such an impact on you.

Here's the hate part: I typically feel overwhelmed by the prospect of remembering and implementing all the tools and techniques offered in these books. Honestly, I often doubt the possibility that I *can* sustain real, lasting change through the very good frameworks and formulas I learn from these books. Most certainly, I doubt that I can digest even five such books a year and make significant, sustainable use of what I've learned.

Which tools should I focus on? Which tools will I remember? Which tools should take priority? Typically, the book I read most recently wins my effort, at least for a while... until I read the next compelling book.

If this experience rings true for you, by now you're overwhelmed by this book, thinking, *I'll never be able to remember the Adhesive strategies or the Binding techniques. I'll never remember how to hook the audience or use metaphors. I'll never remember what to include in a Story Vault. There's just no way.*

To that I say, YOU'RE RIGHT.

You'll never remember all the detailed storytelling frameworks offered in this playbook. Nor will you have time to refine all your stories with every recommended technique. You might not use storytelling often enough to hone your skills. Your team will face competing priorities that will often push storytelling to the back burner.

But if you are convinced that:

- The cause you must advocate for is truly noble,
- Your communication about your cause must engage many components of your audiences' brains, and
- Forest Stories and Tree Tales are the way to activate the hearts and minds of your audiences,

... then I urge you to do two things.

First, select your top three takeaways from this book. What three frameworks, principles, techniques, or strategies could make the biggest impact on you and your team's use of storytelling for advocacy? Maybe you want to keep the Story Loop front and center in you're thinking about how you frame a story. Draw the loop on a sticky note and attach it to your computer monitor. Or perhaps you want your team to implement the frameworks of Tree Tales and Forest Stories. Build a Story Vault that includes those categories, so you and your team are more likely to use those frameworks to strategize about your stories.

Just choose three and let the rest go for now. Take some immediate action that forces you to use the vocabulary (phrases like Tree Tales, Story Loop, Story Vault) and see how your storytelling strategy transforms!

Second, follow these 10 Storytelling Rules to focus on the big principles without sweating the details of every tool and technique outlined in the previous chapters.

10 COMPELLING STORYTELLING RULES

#1 – There Are No Rules

Wow, that's quite a start to a list of rules, right? Yet in truth, storytelling is an art, not a science. While many devices can make a story more compelling, there are no formulas or rules you must follow exactly as I've described them.

While I stand by all I've shared about what elements result in the most compelling narratives, you may find creative ways to use the Story Loop, combine Story Types, or merge Tree Tales and Forest Stories that look a bit different than the examples you've read in this book.

To that I say, GREAT! Go for it, always asking yourself what will speak to your audiences' hearts and minds as you construct your stories.

#2 – Okay, Maybe One Rule: Let Structure Reign

If I'm pressed to offer at least one rule, I would say: Never abandon the Story Loop. Recall from Chapter 4 that a chronology of events isn't a story. An abstract testimonial statement isn't a story. A series of data-packed slides isn't a story.

Your audience's brain is only responding in story mode if you have a structure that establishes a time, place, and characters (Normal) who then experience a problem (Uh-Oh), need a solution (Intervention), and achieve or hope to achieve a better outcome (New Normal). Without making that basic structure clear to the audience, you don't have a story that ignites the brain functions that are critical to your audience's decision-making.

So, let storytelling structure reign!

#3 – Make Simplicity Your Friend

Many people I work with find that once they get started with the Story Loop and then add the Adhesive techniques of vivid details, sensory images, vivid characters, analogies, metaphors, and an opening hook, they are suddenly compelled to elaborate and perfect all the details of the story. I love seeing their enthusiasm.

At the same time, I notice that overusing or inauthentically using these tools can overshadow the heart of the story. People wanting to tell an impactful story for advocacy start to sound like they're trying to become Charles Dickens or Toni Morrison. The metaphors and descriptions start to take over and distract from the real point of the story.

So, keep the story simple. Your goal is to drive action, not to win an Academy Award or the Nobel Prize for literature.

#4 – Don't Assume Your Audience Can't Handle a Good Tree Tale

I often notice myself feeling anxious when I start to describe Tree Tales to "data people," despite all I know and believe from neuroscience. I assume that because they are very data-focused in their work, they're going to think Tree Tales are fluffy, irrelevant, and a waste of time.

But time and time again, I've been amazed at how receptive data-focused audiences are to well-told, relevant, succinct Tree Tales. Once they understand that a Forest Story is the most strategic way to share their data, they consistently confess that their data-heavy Forest Stories would benefit from the insertion of Tree Tales.

So, be smart. Use them sparingly and strategically. But don't hesitate to stir hearts with a good Tree Tale.

#5 – Remember that Stories Are Powerful, But Not Silver Bullets

Two truths:

- Stories affect human decision-making, and you can't afford not to tell them.
- Stories will not always get the exact results you're looking for, and you can't afford to assume they will.

Two truths:
- Stories affect human decision-making, and you can't afford not to tell them.
- Stories will not always get the exact results you're looking for, and you can't afford to assume they will.

An entire chapter of this book was written to convince you from neuroscience research that storytelling is essential to your advocacy work. I believe it and hope you do too.

I also know that hundreds of variables are at play when humans make decisions to act, or not, on our requests.

You have competition.

You're asking for something from your audience in support of your cause: time, resources, investment, policy changes, behavior changes. But other entities are also asking for those same resources, and while you may have a compelling story, your competitors may have an equally compelling story that better aligns with the audience's values or priorities.

History, culture, politics, religion, worldview, personal experience, psychology, biology, genetics — even whether your audience is hungry (seriously) — all contribute to their decisions to act, or not, in support of your cause.[38]

Storytelling is not a silver bullet. At the same time, it's a tool you can't afford to ignore.

#6 – *Tell Your Story Over and Over Again*

Because of the competing variables mentioned in Rule #5, you may need to tell your story multiple times in multiple ways before you get the action you're seeking. Your audience may not be convinced after hearing the story once, but after they hear it multiple times, it may come to have more weight.

Because a multitude of variables are at play, be prepared to tell your story many times over.[39] You are not defeated if your story doesn't drive action immediately. Modify, edit, adapt, and keep telling it!

#7 – *Let Go of a Good Story When It's Time*

Many of my clients need to continually add to their story repertoire. After all, you don't want the audiences you face repeatedly thinking, "Oh yeah, we've heard this one a million times."

The Indianapolis Children's Choir, referred to in Chapter 3, made great use of their Hurdle Story to demonstrate their innovation during the COVID-19 pandemic and inspire donors to contribute generously to the organization, ensuring their survival. However, the Hurdle Story quickly became irrelevant to the donors once the children were singing together in person again. No longer were they moved by the remarkable adaptation. They wanted to hear stories of current impact.

While you may love a story in your Story Vault that is powerful, compelling, and inspiring, ask yourself whether it's time to lay that story to rest for the sake of your mission.

#8 – *Let the Process Teach You About Your Noble Cause*

Sometimes we don't know the meaning or value of our experiences until we express them in the form of a story.

When I told stories at the children's hospital and had the experience of telling *The Three Little Pigs* to the little girl who was moaning from her pain, I didn't realize at the time how that night impacted me until I sat down to describe that event using the Story Loop. Only then did I realize what I had learned from that experience about the power of storytelling.

Crafting the story clarified *my* New Normal.

You, too, will gain clarity about your mission through the very act of shaping your story.

#9 – *You ARE a Storyteller, So Enjoy the Telling*

If only I had a dollar for every time someone has told me they're not a good storyteller. Oh, how wealthy I would be.

People often believe they're not good storytellers because they hold a mental image of someone in their life who is a natural-born storyteller. Grandma Ruth is the family storyteller who captivates everyone at the Thanksgiving table. Or Uncle Fred was the one who could spin a tale around the campfire, keeping everyone on the edges of their seats.

But the truth is, you, too, are a storyteller. When something goes awry, you tell someone the story with an Uh-Oh moment, keeping your friends and family on the edge of their seats.

What's new here is that you're becoming aware of yourself as a storyteller, telling stories for a strategic purpose, and considering the needs and interests of your audience. Yes, that changes things, but you *can* learn to modify what you already do naturally and make it strategic.

You are a storyteller already! Enjoy the process.

#10 – *Stories Can Be Dangerous; Tell the Truth*

Stories are powerful, which means stories are dangerous.

Stories can easily be fabricated, especially through social media. And stories can be manipulated, misrepresenting the truth of a matter.

Details omitted from a Tree Tale might cause an audience to feel more sympathetic to a character or organization than is warranted. Data can be manipulated in a Forest Story, preventing an audience from seeing the entire "forest."

The problem of fabrication and exaggeration comes with no easy solutions. After all, your truth may be in direct opposition to someone else's truth.

So please know this: Storytelling is serious, ethical business. It is up to you to treat these frameworks and tools with utmost responsibility, care, and honesty. I hope for nothing less.

> Storytelling is serious, ethical business. It is up to you to treat these frameworks and tools with utmost responsibility, care, and honesty.

ONE FINAL NOTE: USE AI WITH CAUTION

As much as anyone else, I love, use, and marvel at the content ChatGPT spits out.

Can it help you tell your story more effectively? Absolutely. Should it replace your efforts to craft your story? Absolutely not. Especially if you are the one to deliver your story.

While ChatGPT or any other AI tool may help lead you to the right words, a useful metaphor, or a better way to explain your data, when you go to tell the story, it needs to sound like you. Only you or the original source of a story — especially a Tree Tale — know the vivid details from the original experience. ChatGPT can neither generate those details nor recall them the way you see them in your mind's eye.

If you're delivering ChatGPT's version of your story orally, your audience will sense the inauthenticity in your voice. Suddenly, you're reading or memorizing the words of another entity, and you'll likely struggle to get the words right because they're not yours.

Authenticity influences the credibility of your story and, ultimately, that of your noble cause. So, yes, use AI to help refine your story, but avoid letting it replace your voice and your humanity.

THE COMPELLING POWER AT YOUR FINGERTIPS

You have a cause worth advancing. You need support for that cause. You must influence your audiences to *decide* to act in support of your cause.

By implementing with your team the frameworks and techniques you've read in these pages, I guarantee that you will be able to say:

- My team and I are fueling our advocacy with strategically designed stories.
- We have a coherent storytelling strategy guiding all our stakeholder communications.
- We use the storytelling frameworks of Story Types, Story Loop, Tree Tales, Forest Stories, and more to talk about our strategy.
- We have a robust Story Vault, documenting how, when, and why we're using stories.
- We actively use the Story Vault for efficiency and clarity of direction, no longer duplicating efforts, but taking advantage of one another's stories to continue building and adapting stories strategically.
- I am actively reinforcing and modifying the vision with stories of my own.

While a multitude of variables will impact the mileage you get from your storytelling, using the frameworks and techniques in this book will improve your chances of driving stakeholder action in support of your efforts, increasing the possibility that you can say, *We've gained support and can make a difference like never before.*

This is the potential you now hold in your hands.

Using the frameworks and techniques in this book will improve your chances of driving stakeholder action in support of your efforts, increasing the possibility that you can say, *We've gained support and can make a difference like never before.*

Given the challenges you face in persuading your audiences to take the action you need, the sooner you put these frameworks to use, the better.

Jump into the work, using these frameworks and tools to engage minds and stir hearts. Then watch your world change as you and your noble cause move from story to action.

END NOTES

1   Granville N. Toogood, *The Articulate Executive in Action: How the Best Leaders Get Things Done* (McGraw-Hill, 2005).

2   Sam Dabir, "The Neuroscience of Decision Making," *Thrive Online*, April 2024, https://www.uwo.ca/se/thrive/blog/2024/the-neuroscience-of-decision-making.html.

3   Neuroscience Foundation, "The Neuroscience Behind Decision-Making," *Neuroscience Foundation*, accessed March 30, 2025, https://www.neurosciencefoundation.org/post/the-neuroscience-behind-decision-making.

4   Aron K. Barbey, Michael Koenigs, and Jordan Grafman, "Dorsolateral Prefrontal Contributions to Human Working Memory," *Cortex* 49, no. 5 (May 2013): 1195–1205, https://doi.org/10.1016/j.cortex.2012.05.022.

5   Amy F. T. Arnsten, "The Neurobiology of Thought: The Groundbreaking Discoveries of Patricia Goldman-Rakic (1937–2003)," *Cerebral Cortex* 23, no. 10 (October 2013): 2269–2281, https://doi.org/10.1093/cercor/bht195.

6   *NeuroLaunch* Editorial Team, "Brain Regions Controlling Decision Making: Unraveling the Neural Networks," *NeuroLaunch*, September 30, 2024, https://neurolaunch.com/what-part-of-the-brain-controls-decision-making/.

7   *NeuroLaunch* Editorial Team, "Brain Regions."

8   Robert C. Malenka, Eric J. Nestler, and Steven E. Hyman, *Molecular Neuropharmacology: A Foundation for Clinical Neuroscience*, ed. Arvid Sydor and Ronald Y. Brown, 2nd ed. (McGraw-Hill Medical, 2009), 147–148, 367, 376.

9   "Where Is Decision Making in the Brain?" *The Cognitive Mind*, accessed March 30, 2025, https://thecognitivemind. com/where-is-decision-making-in-the-brain/.

10 *NeuroLaunch* Editorial Team, "Brain Regions."

11 Okinawa Institute of Science and Technology, "Mapping the Decision-Making Pathways in the Brain," *Neuroscience News*, September 18, 2020, https://neurosciencenews.com/ decision-making-brain-17051/.

12 Okinawa Institute of Science and Technology, "Mapping the Decision-Making."

13 Brendan I. Cohn-Sheehy and Charan Ranganath, "Hippocampus Is the Brain's Storyteller," *Current Biology* 31, no. 19 (September 27, 2021): R1245–R1246, https://doi. org/10.1016/j.cub.2021.08.078.

14 *NeuroLaunch* Editorial Team, "Storytelling's Impact on the Brain: Neuroscience Behind Narrative Power," *NeuroLaunch*, September 30, 2024, https://neurolaunch. com/how-storytelling-affects-the-brain/.

15 NeuroLeadership Institute, "The Neuroscience of Storytelling," *Your Brain at Work*, September 30, 2021, https://neuroleadership.com/your-brain-at-work/ the-neuroscience-of-storytelling/.

16 Paul J. Zak, "Why Inspiring Stories Make Us React: The Neuroscience of Narrative," *Cerebrum*, February 2, 2015, https://www.dana.org/article/why-inspiring-stories-make- us-react-the-neuroscience-of-narrative/.

17 Paul J. Zak, "Why Inspiring Stories."

18 Uri Hasson et al., "Brain-to-Brain Coupling: A Mechanism for Creating and Sharing a Social World," *Trends in Cognitive Sciences* 16, no. 2 (2012): 114–121.

19 Greg J. Stephens, Lauren J. Silbert, and Uri Hasson, "Speaker-Listener Neural Coupling Underlies Successful Communication," *Proceedings of the National Academy of Sciences* 107, no. 32 (2010): 14425–14430, https://doi.org/10.1073/pnas.1008662107.

20 Helen Branswell, "A Nightmarish Tale: Unvaccinated Boy's Tetanus Infection Was First in 30 Years in Oregon," *STAT*, March 7, 2019, https://www.statnews.com/2019/03/07/nightmarish-tale-tetanus-unvaccinated-child/.

21 Robert M. Sapolsky, *Behave: The Biology of Humans at Our Best and Worst* (Penguin Press, 2017).

22 Robert Sapolsky, *Behave*.

23 Reviews were on the Omni Hotels website, but have since been removed after a site update. Current site URL is https://www.omnihotels.com/hotels/amelia-island.

24 Gustav Freytag, *Freytag's Technique of the Drama: An Exposition of Dramatic Composition and Art*, trans. Elias J. MacEwan (Scott, Foresman and Company, 1894).

25 Eugene L. Lowry, *The Homiletical Plot: The Sermon as Narrative Art Form*, expanded ed. (Westminster John Knox Press, 2001). The Story Loop is adapted from the "Lowry Loop," a narrative model for sermons. Lowry lays out five stages of the sermon loop: "Oops," "Ugh," "Aha," "Whee," and "Yeah" which take the listener through a problem, a turning point or insight, a good-news solution, and implications for the listener's life.

26 I was first introduced to the idea of the Story Loop model by master storyteller Donald Davis. I am indebted to him for giving me a version of this model that taught me how to tell a compelling story.

27 All details have been changed for anonymization of this story.

28 All data and details have been changed for anonymization.

29 **Paul J. Zak, "Why Inspiring Stories."**

30 Jorge A. Barraza et al., "The Heart of the Story: Peripheral Physiology During Narrative Exposure Predicts Charitable Giving," *Biological Psychology* 105 (2015): 138–143, https://doi.org/10.1016/j.biopsycho.2015.01.008.

31 Paul Jenkins, "Neuroscience of Storytelling: Unraveling the Brain's Narrative Processing," *Brilliantio*, April 6, 2024, https://brilliantio.com/neuroscience-of-storytelling/.

32 Paul Jenkins, "Neuroscience of Storytelling."

33 Cole Nussbaumer Knaflic, *Storytelling with Data: A Data Visualization Guide for Business Professionals* (Wiley, 2015).

34 Kathryn A. Whitehead, *"Tiny Balls of Fat That Could Revolutionize Medicine,"* TED, filmed April 2021 at TED@DuPont, video, 10:50, https://www.ted.com/talks/kathryn_a_whitehead_tiny_balls_of_fat_that_could_revo-lutionize_medicine.

35 John Medina, *Brain Rules: 12 Principles for Surviving and Thriving at Work, Home, and School* (Pear Press, 2008).

36 Vanessa Van Edwards, *You Are Contagious*, TEDxLondon, June 4, 2017, video, 18:17, https://www.youtube.com/watch?v=cef35Fk7YD8.

37 Matthew Dicks, *Storyworthy: Engage, Teach, Persuade, and Change Your Life Through the Power of Storytelling* (New World Library, 2018).

38 S. Danziger, J. Levav, and L. Avnaim-Pesso, "Extraneous factors in judicial decisions," *Proceedings of the National Academy of Sciences* 108 no. 17 (2011): 6889–6892.

39 Robert M. Sapolsky, *Behave.*

ACKNOWLEDGEMENTS

I didn't know 20 years ago that I was preparing to write a book, but I know today that *From Story to Action* would not be in your hands without the tutelage, wisdom, editing, and loving support of so many people. Here's my story of gratitude.

Once upon a time, over 20 years ago, I attended a Storytelling Arts of Indiana event at the Indianapolis Children's Museum with my kids. It changed my life. There, I met **Ellen Munds,** former Executive Director of SAI, who came to believe in me, affording me countless opportunities to hone my craft as a storyteller on stage and as a trainer. Through Ellen, I met my first story mentor, **Carol Brown**, with whom I told *The Three Little Pigs* to the precious girl in the hospital.

Through Ellen Munds, I met dozens of nationally acclaimed storytellers whose work has inspired and instructed me over the years. Most notably, I benefited from the wise coaching of **Beth Horner**, who has spent hours critiquing my storytelling performances, teaching me how to make stories relevant and sticky with audiences, and helping me get out of my head and into the minds of my audience.

I'm also indebted to master storyteller **Donald Davis**, who first exposed me to the notion of a "loop" story structure rooted in homiletics. Envisioning story structure as a loop rather than the traditional rising climax has been the single most influential storytelling framework in my work. I'm grateful to Donald Davis and share his delight that his work lives on in this book.

My journey in storytelling unexpectedly led me to the tech industry, where I've had an extraordinary education in strategic storytelling for business from **Amy Brown**, Founder and CEO of **Authenticx**, a tech company built on AI innovation that helps humans understand humans in the healthcare industry. I'm indebted to Amy for the opportunity to invent a role called "insights storyteller," develop methods for telling data-backed stories, and cultivate a team of storytellers who are making AI-generated data accessible and persuasive to healthcare leaders who want to improve patient experience. I'm so blessed to work with Amy, **Kip Zurcher** (CFO), my outstanding team of **insights storytellers**, and the entire company of **Authentizens** who have helped sponsor and school me in this work. These are people who understand the power of Tree Tales and Forest Stories like no other.

Naturally, this book is filled with stories from noble clients and colleagues who generously agreed to let me share their stories so that others might learn. The list includes **Emily Bopp** (chief of staff) and **Chris Fredericks** (CEO) of Empowered Ventures; **Mark Medvitz** and **Andrea Preuss**; **Joshua Pedde**, artistic director of the Indianapolis Children's Choir; **Ruth Church**, founder of Artisan Coffee Imports; **Pat Padgett**, executive VP of the Kentucky Medical Association; **physician participants** in the Kentucky Physician Leadership Institute; and **Kip Zurcher**, CFO of Authenticx. Each of their stories offered clarity and proof that compelling stories make a difference.

Thanks also go to **Megan Kendall** for her beautiful photography and **Tessa McKenney** for transforming my chicken-scratch drawings into aesthetically pleasing, highly illustrative graphics.

The sheer courage to write this book came from my interaction with hundreds of clients over the years who have affirmed the value of the frameworks and tools I've taught them in trainings and workshops. I am indebted to the thousands of leaders and teams with noble causes who have expressed their gratitude for the contents of this book. Along with those clients, I've been fortunate to encounter colleagues over the years who have codified their own ideas in their books and encouraged me to do the same. My thanks go to authors **Karen Lisko**, **Andy Black**, **Kris Taylor**, **Julie Kratz**, **Caroline Dowd-Higgens**, and **Dora Lutz**, who blazed the book authorship trail for me.

The work would have created a terrible Uh-Oh with the contents of this book without the first-class strategic coaching of **Nicole Gebhardt** of Niche Pressworks. Nicole was my fairy godmother who worked her magic to shift my academic mindset to the more practical, business mindset needed by my readers. **Kim Han** has been an exceptional project manager, keeping me on track with deadlines and logistics. I'm indebted to **Tami** for her beautifully imaginative cover design and her patience with me and my ever-changing title. And I owe more thanks than I can muster to **Melanie,** who has been an editor extraordinaire. When your editor is willing to say, "that's just a weird phrase" (Uh-Oh!), you can trust you're getting the honest, direct feedback you need. I couldn't have been luckier than to land Melanie with her clarity of mind and vision to see what I could not throughout the writing journey.

I've often joked that writing this book was an investment in lattes. I'm grateful for the quiet working space at Normal Coffee at the Tube Factory in Indianapolis — a hidden gem of an arts center — and the delicious lattes prepared for me by **Lauren,** who, alongside **Sylvia,** cheered me on week after week as I wrote at my "satellite office" by the window.

I am grateful to those in my inner circle who have conveyed their belief in me and this project. My dear and deep friend **Mary Katherine** challenges my thinking upon every conversation and is responsible for exposing me to the intellectual giant Robert Sapolsky, whose work has tamed my assumptions about the limitless power of storytelling.

My two figurative sisters, **Karen** and **Marsha,** inspire me to do hard things, ask yet another question, dream vividly, give generously, and occasionally wear a costume in airports just to make people laugh. I wouldn't have written this had Karen not simultaneously been writing her excellent book, *Kind Dynamite*, with Marsha cheering us both on.

My two literal sisters, **Judy** and **Nancy**, nurtured me as a storyteller when I was young. Judy acted out stories on stage. And before I could read, Nancy helped me memorize a Bible story word-for-word to tell our children's church group. I suspect that was the catalyst for what I do now. We're all three grateful to our beloved parents, **Jean and Forest Perkins**, who read us storybooks and passed along family stories as we sat on the back patio sipping iced tea on summer evenings.

The characters in my story who have been the most supportive and influential are those in my precious family. Our wise-beyond-their-years adult kids, **Kendra** and **Elliott**, grew up listening to me tell ghost stories, folk tales, family stories, and historical stories, and now I'm lucky enough to be expanded by their amazing life stories, which enrich me beyond what I could ever fathom.

And most of all, the best character in my life is my dear husband **Jim**, the King of Analogies, who has sacrificed more than anyone for this project. He has gifted me with unyielding love and support ever since I entered the unorthodox work of storytelling, always saying "go for it," always providing poignant feedback, always providing loads of laughter at just the right moments. I would choose no one else to create a lifetime of stories with. I'm so fortunate.

Thank *you*, reader, for the noble work you are doing and your desire to drive action that will make the world a better place. It's my sincere wish that the frameworks and techniques in this book take you and your cause from *story to action*.

ABOUT SALLY PERKINS

Building on her 30-year academic career in rhetorical studies and her 20 years as a story performer, Dr. Sally Perkins has equipped hundreds of clients with easy-to-use storytelling frameworks that give them a strategic edge in their ability to champion their noble causes. Clients have included, among others: United Way, American Cancer Society, Union Pacific Railroad, Bell's Brewery, Crane Army Ammunition, Indiana and Kentucky physicians and health advocates, Butler University, Augusta University, and numerous others. She also coaches individuals preparing for keynote speeches, TEDx talks, and other public speaking events.

Sally serves as senior manager of insight storytellers at *Authenticx,* an Indianapolis-based AI company. There, she weaves data into compelling stories that drive patient-centric change in healthcare. She was a recipient of the TechPoint 2021 Tech 25 Award for her pioneering work as an insights data-backed storyteller.

When not training or telling data-backed stories, Sally performs stories of all sorts — historical, wisdom-based, personal, and ghoulish — to audiences of all ages. She has performed for the United Solo Theatre Festival Off-Broadway, the National Storytelling Network, the Indianapolis Spirit and Place Festival, the Tennessee Haunting in the Hills Festival, the Crown Hill Cemetery Festival of Ghost Stories, and the Indy Fringe Theatre Festival. After seeing her one-woman show Digging in Their Heels off-Broadway, a reviewer referred to her as, "the consummate performer and teacher. She is inspirational and clever and knows how to engage the audience from start to finish."

Holding a Ph.D. in rhetorical studies, Sally has taught and published in the field of rhetoric and public speaking for over 30 years. She has taught at the University of Kansas, California State University-Sacramento, and Butler University, receiving numerous awards for outstanding teaching.

While she loves equipping her clients and performing stories on stage, the most important stories she tells are those at the bedsides of kids at Riley's Hospital for Children in Indianapolis.

CONTACT

Website: SallyPerkins.net
LinkedIn: LinkedIn.com/in/sally-perkins-sjp/
Facebook: Sally.Perkins.1217
Instagram: @SallyPerkins590

www.ingramcontent.com/pod-product-compliance
Lightning Source LLC
Chambersburg PA
CBHW071603210326
41597CB00019B/3375